Singing
Professionally

Singing Professionally

STUDYING

SINGING

FOR

ACTORS

AND

SINGERS

Arabella Hong Young

HEINEMANN
Portsmouth, New Hampshire

HEINEMANN
A division of Reed Elsevier Inc.
361 Hanover Street Portsmouth, NH 03801-3912
Offices and agents throughout the world

Every effort has been made to contact the copyright holders for permission to reprint borrowed material where necessary. We regret any oversights that may have occurred and would be happy to rectify them in future printings of this work.

The author and publisher are grateful to the following for permission to reprint previously published material:

Figure 2–1 *Vocal Apparatus* from *The Anatomy Coloring Book* by Wynn Kapit and Lawrence M. Elson. Copyright © 1977 by Wynn Kapit and Lawrence M. Elson. Reprinted by permission of HarperCollins Publishers, Inc.

Figure 2–4 from *An Outline of English Phonetics* by David Jones. Copyright 1918 by David Jones, 1940 renewed. Used by permission of Dutton Signet, a division of Penguin Books USA Inc.

Library of Congress Cataloging-in-Publication Data
Young, Arabella Hong.
    Singing professionally : studying singing for actors and singers /
Arabella Hong Young.
        p. cm.
    ISBN 0–435–08677–4 (acid-free paper)
    1. Singing—Instruction and study. I. Title.
MT820.Y68 1995
783'.043—dc20   95-17856
                                                                                                CIP
                                                                                                MN

Editor: Lisa Barnett
Production: JB Tranchemontagne
Design: Joni Doherty
Cover design: Mary Cronin
Back cover photo by Roy Blakey

Printed in the United States of America on acid-free paper

Docutech RRD 2002

I
dedicate this book to my husband
for all his wise advice
and skillful help.

Contents

Part One ℘ Beginner's Technique

Illustrations

Foreword

To some degree, we all know how to sing, but to improve we must delve into the mechanics of singing. Although singing in the shower is simple and fun, singing onstage creates anxiety. Unless you are trained in the techniques of singing, your voice shakes and you wonder if you will even get the first note out. You must learn the technique of singing. This involves developing proper body posture for breath control, placing the voice in various registers, using resonance for projection, and interpreting lyrics. Even more vocal training is required to reach the highest level of competency.

The techniques used in this book are mainly for musical theater. Classical students, however, can find them helpful as well. They can help the actor sing a simple tune or an operatic role. Opera singers can find it useful as a classical technique as well as a vocal approach more suitable for musical theater. Techniques range from the simplest approach for beginners to advanced study for serious students.

Acknowledgments

I wish to thank Lisa Barnett
for inviting me to write this book.
She has given me the opportunity to bring together
30 years of teaching singing.

I am most grateful to Michael Brown
for his astute advice on style in writing.

Linda Carroll has been an inspiration
in her scientific vocal expertise.

Dorothy Bradburg's refinements in English
have been most helpful.

Introduction

Technique makes the difference between the professional and the amateur. The book is divided into three levels: Beginner's Technique, Intermediate Technique, and Advanced Technique.

The first sections on Beginner's and Intermediate Vocal Technique give you a basic foundation for voice production. Advanced Vocal Technique covers a more fully developed singing such as coloratura singing, falsetto singing and adapting the opera voice to musical theater. The subjects of acting, auditioning, and Zen in the Art of Studying Singing could be separate books in themselves. In this book only an introduction is presented in order to show their effect on Advanced Vocal Production.

This book is best used with an instructor because while you can gain a lot of technical understanding from a book, you must be guided in order to apply the technique and exercises correctly.

CHOOSING A TEACHER

Select a voice teacher rather than a vocal coach. The difference between the two is that a voice teacher develops the voice in quality, size, range, and control through exercises, while a coach works on repertoire, coloration, phrasing, style, and interpretation.

You can start with a voice teacher first, and add a vocal coach later. Some teachers do both; this can be helpful since methods often differ from one teacher to another and can be confusing.

Teachers usually employ methods based on Italian and German techniques. To implement these methods, they use images. This visualization of sound as an umbrella or mushroom provides a physical formation of the breath that shapes vocal muscles and positions the larynx for production of sound. The larynx or voice box is an involuntary apparatus that can be controlled by the surrounding muscles of the mouth, tongue, soft palate, and jaw through a coordinated effort of imaging. For example, the image of singing down to your toes helps to produce greater depth of tone, and the umbrella image helps to provide more overtones. At the same time that the larynx produces the fundamental sound, it is the pharynx—at the soft palate in the back part of the mouth—that provides the quality and overtones of the sound.

With the advent of scientific instruments, we can now examine the vocal elements from a physiological basis. For instance, in examining how the vocal folds vibrate, we can determine their effect on the quality of sound. Also, we can objectively examine the effects of posture in different types of breathing and so forth. Scientific research has also clarified the mysteries of images and has brought the whole method of singing to a higher level of understanding.

USING THIS BOOK

This book combines images with the scientific approach. Physiological explanations are given in simple terms that explain the mechanical procedures that accompany the use of images.

In this book a variety of classical vocal methods are combined to form a single method that has been adapted for singing in musical theater. This adaptation is important, since many who study vocal technique with an opera teacher and repertoire with a theater coach find that the classical technique is quite different from that of musical theater: The pure chest voice is forbidden for operatic sopranos, whereas, in musical theater, it is the basis of vocal production.

Classical techniques used in this adaptation include the Italian Method for the clarity of vowels, the legato line, and the mask technique to add a ring to the voice. The German Method helps enrich tone through the pucker technique, and the Chewing Method is used for hygienic production and relief of tension in the voice.

This method provides a practical and integrated technique for better vocal quality and control to those aspiring to sing on Broadway.

This integrated technique of three different methods allows you to adjust to the vocal needs of each style. The proper method for individual types of songs is pointed out in the introduction of each technique. Many coaches teach only one approach; however, be open to various methods in your learning attitude. All of the experiences that you gain in all kinds of studies can benefit you in the future without your being aware of them at the time.

When I was a student at Juilliard, I was very much into the mask technique that produced brilliance and agility for me. In fact it did so much for me, when I graduated, I won three of the major grants in classical singing that year: They gave me a New York Debut Recital, a concert tour in Europe, and an appearance as soloist with the Thomas Scherman Orchestra in New York. Sustaining was hard for me because I just used the mask technique. Later on when I learned the pucker technique, it gave me a deeper sound and support and helped tremendously in the change of voice so that I was able to sustain more easily. I also had to take harmony classes at Juilliard, which I thought was a waste of time. Much later when I had my act, I was able to copy all of the instrumental parts for the orchestra, saving myself thousands of dollars. Harmony has also been a necessary aid in my teaching. I can show my students how to transpose a song into their own key. So be open to all techniques and experiences; learn from whatever you do. Nothing is lost.

THE METHOD

Requirements

The first requirements in studying singing are a natural voice of quality and the ability to hear pitches. In addition, you need to be able to discern qualities of sound (coloration and richness), intensity (loudness), and phrasing (dynamics and groupings of notes).

With these natural gifts, you can develop the voice through vocal techniques that improve its quality, size, and range. Not only is vocal technique necessary to improve sound, but it is also important to acquire skill for overcoming challenging situations like singing when ill or stressed, or when dealing with vocal problems. Advanced levels require understanding the vocal techniques of many different styles such as opera, pop, rock, and jazz—each demanding a variation on the fundamental approach.

Technique

The basic method for singing consists of proper posture, breath control, voice placement, registration, resonance, and projection. These elements may be studied and developed separately, but in the end they must be combined to operate together as a unified and integrated whole.

Technique starts with proper posture or body alignment as a foundation for breath support. Once the body is centered and breathing is correct, voice placement can follow by the proper positioning muscles of the mouth, tongue, soft palate, and jaw to produce vocal sounds.

The three different registers in the voice are low, middle, and high. As sound proceeds from the lower range through the middle and into the high register, the muscles that control the apparatus for voice placement must adjust to ensure smooth transition. This is similar to changing gears in a car and is called *registration.*

Correct posture, breathing, placement, and registration result in *resonance,* a sympathetic vibration that supports and amplifies the voice in the cavities of the throat, mouth, head, and chest. Resonance gives quality and size to the voice. Adding volume—breath pressure—produces the added carrying power of *projection.*

Study Format

Learning to sing is a complicated process. To simplify the procedure, the steps in each section of study are explained in detail in the exercises. To help in visualizing these steps easily, a *summary* is given at the end of each exercise.

The summary encapsulates all of the steps in a few words to make them immediately available. Imagining each step as if it were actually being used helps to recall the physical procedure more efficiently.

Beginner's Technique

1

Breath Support

Breath support is the foundation in singing—
it is the substance of the voice
and supplies body and strength.

℘

The foundation for singing is correct breath support, controlled by proper posture or body alignment. The breathing apparatus consists of the lungs, diaphragm, and lower abdomen. See Figure 1–1.

The diaphragm is a sheet of muscle connected to the bottom of the lungs. It expands downward to inhale; it relaxes upwards for exhalation and singing. The chest, the back, and lower abdominal muscles control the breathing. This is why it is important to keep a straight alignment of the body. The chest should not be allowed to cave in because the muscles surrounding the rib cage, the back, and the lower abdomen support the

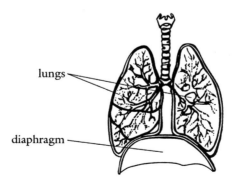

FIGURE 1–1. **The lungs and diaphragm.**

breath. The breathing apparatus is like a drum turned upside down, with the diaphragm the head of the drum and the ribs in front and back making the frame. The ribs must be held upright so that the chest and abdominal muscles can frame and support the sound. Current theory on breath support in singing states that the diaphragm does not support sound, as once believed, but that the chest, back, and lower abdominal muscles control exhalation while the diaphragm merely expands downward during inhalation and then relaxes.

The secret of correct breath support is to maintain an aligned posture so that the chest, back, and lower abdominal muscles can provide support. This explains the upright appearance of opera singers and Shakespearean actors. Maintaining a straight posture may seem awkward at first, but proper alignment of the body will eventually feel relaxed. Proper posture and lower abdominal breathing not only help to control breath and thus the voice, but they also have a calming influence for those who are excited or nervous before stepping onstage.

▮▮▮ POSTURE EXERCISE

1. To achieve the proper posture for singing, stand against a wall and place the heels about two inches from the wall while pushing the small of the back against or near the wall. Straighten the back as much as possible but be comfortable.
2. As you press the small of the back toward the wall to straighten the spine, tuck the buttocks under. The chest should come up and the shoulders should move back without straining. This straightness gives you the proper alignment for singing.

BREATH CONTROL

Once the body becomes properly aligned, the next step is breath control. Breathing properly is breathing reflexively—naturally with no conscious effort. Do not force the lungs to expand by consciously stretching the chest and abdominal muscles. Such forcing causes excessive tension and strain.

For the first step in breathing reflexively, review Figure 1–1 of the lungs and diaphragm. As noted earlier, the diaphragm, which expands downward to inhale and relaxes to exhale, was formerly thought to control the sound so that singers were told to breathe diaphragmatically. We now know that it is the chest, back muscles, and lower abdomen that control exhalation and produce the sound. Only when posture is erect are the chest, back muscles, and lower abdomen aligned to support the breath.

▪▪▪ BREATHING EXERCISE

With posture properly aligned, try this exercise in reflexive breathing. Exhale by standing straight and expelling air from the lungs. Maintaining this posture after exhaling completely leads to inhaling both reflexively and fully.

Exhalation

1. Stand in an erect posture.
2. Place your hand on the lower abdominal area.
3. Open the mouth and exhale slowly with a barely audible "ha" sound.
4. While expelling all the air, keep the chest up and pull the lower abdomen in by following the breath out gently. Gradually continue with the surrounding muscles (the sides around the waist and also muscles in the small of the back).

Exhaling causes the diaphragm to rise like a balloon and the muscles of the rib cage to compress, both expelling the air—as in ordinary breathing. In singing, however, with the chest kept high, muscles of the inner and outer rib cage and lower abdomen give greater support and control for the exhaling breath to produce sound. This is proper posture, as opposed to letting the chest cave in and losing support of the breath in a so-called relaxed position with the shoulders drooping forward and chest down.

At the bottom of a breath there is more breath left in the lungs.

5. To exhale completely make a hissing sound with the letter *s* and expel the rest of the air by following the breath out gently while pulling the lower abdomen in and keeping the chest up. You can pull the buttocks under and tighten the legs for further support.

All movement should be gentle; follow the breath out without excessive force. Be sure to keep the chest up.

More complete exhaling means more fully inhaling. The greater the vacuum created in the lungs, the greater the atmospheric pressure to provide air.

Inhalation

1. Exhaling properly, wait for a count of 2.
2. Open the throat by relaxing it and allow air to fill the lungs by following the breath in. Inhale through the nose and barely parted lips; the breathing will not be visible.

During inhaling, the diaphragm contracts downward while the rib cage and waist area around the body expand like a bellows, as shown in Figure 1–2. The feeling is breathing in a down-and-out motion.

Singing in a slow tempo allows air to be taken in through the nose alone, but when the music is fast, air needs to enter through the nose *and* mouth. Taking a quick breath just through the nose while using a microphone makes a sound like a vacuum cleaner. Even experienced opera singers can seem to be doing a breathing exercise when inhaling audibly using only the nose.

At the beginning of practice do the breathing exercise five times before actually vocalizing, resting between each repetition. Not being used to so much oxygen may cause slight dizziness at first, but this will disappear.

This exercise is also good for calming nerves before an audition, going onstage, or when emotionally upset.

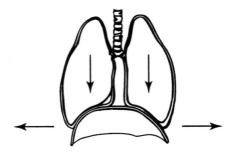

FIGURE 1–2. Down-and-out movement during inhalation.

Full exhalation is very important: the fuller the exhalation the bigger the inhalation, because a greater vacuum in the lungs makes outside air push in more forcefully. Since the procedure is reflexive, it allows spontaneous breathing without excessive tension.

Proper breath support is the foundation for the voice. At the same time that it supports, sustains, and controls production, it also keeps the voice from shaking.

Summary
1. Exhale reflexively
2. Inhale reflexively with an expansive down-and-out direction.
   (The diaphragm goes down as the ribs go out.)

2

Voice Placement

Placement is the focus of the voice.
It is the key that opens the door
to quality and range.

℘

Vocal technique is the development of skills that produce quality, range, and control. The two most important technical elements in the method are breath support and voice placement.

PLACEMENT

Voice placement is achieved by positioning the muscles of the mouth, tongue, soft palate, and jaw. These are the tools of the singer. They control the *larynx*—the voice box at the Adam's Apple. The larynx makes the fundamental sound. Above the larynx lies the soft palate or *pharynx*. The pharynx provides resonance or quality. See Figure 2–1 for the location of the larynx, pharynx, and *vocal folds,* or cords. Lines are drawn from the vocal folds to different views of the larynx.

We all know the location of the tongue, mouth, and jaw, but awareness of the soft palate in relation to the tongue and vocal folds is important in understanding where and how the sound is produced. This is explained in detail in the following section.

Vowels are building blocks of the voice: They determine coloration—specific quality—and assist in placement. Sound is created by vocal folds on top of the larynx and from there travels up into the cavities of the head to be shaped into vowels in the pharynx. Sound is controlled by positioning muscles of the mouth, tongue, soft palate, and jaw. It also is influenced by the use of vowels that cause the muscles to form different shapes of space inside the mouth.

Distinct harmonic overtones are made when varied vowel shapes direct the breath into different parts of the mouth to give a variety of richness to the voice.

BREATH DIRECTION

Breath direction controls quality, resonance, and volume. Since harmonic overtones are made by directing the breath into different parts of the mouth, you can control the sound by where you direct your breath.

As illustrated in Figure 2–2, when the breath is directed above the center-of-placement line (see arrow in diagram) the *head voice* is produced;

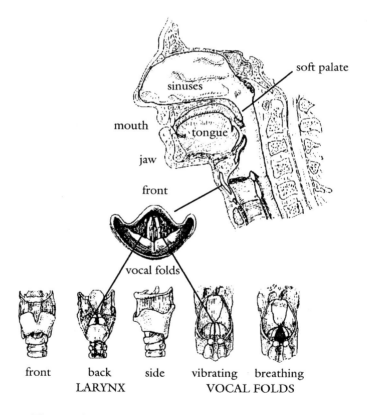

FIGURE 2–1. The vocal apparatus.

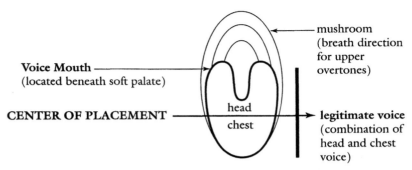

BREATH IN UPPER REGISTER

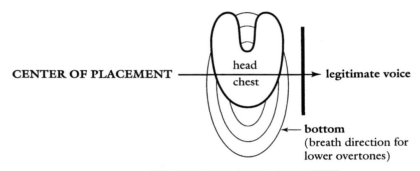

BREATH IN LOWER REGISTER

FIGURE 2–2. Center of placement and effect of breath direction.

and when it is directed below the center of the line, the *chest voice* is attained. Like a stereo system, the head is the treble and the chest is the bass of a voice.

Directing the breath simultaneously above and below the center line produces a *legitimate* voice, like the mixture of head and chest found in the sounds used by Rodgers and Hammerstein and by Lerner and Loewe. Using all resonators of the throat, mouth, head, and chest fortifies breath direction and produces the *opera voice*.

Stay at the center of placement throughout the upper and lower register to maintain treble and bass qualities throughout the range. When going higher, use fewer low overtones (indicated by the bottom in the chart) and when going lower, fewer high overtones (identified by the mushroom in the diagram). The tendency to lift above the center line when rising produces a falsetto quality; pushing below the line when dropping makes a muddy quality. Such lifting and pushing down strains the voice.

CHANGE OF BREATH DIRECTION
THROUGHOUT THE RANGE

Figure 2–3 shows how breath direction changes in different registers:

The lower register is indicated in small letters.

The middle range is in capital letters.

The high range is in capital letters with the number 1.

The extreme high register is in capital letters with the number 2.

Middle C is designated with the capital letter and high C is marked High C^2.

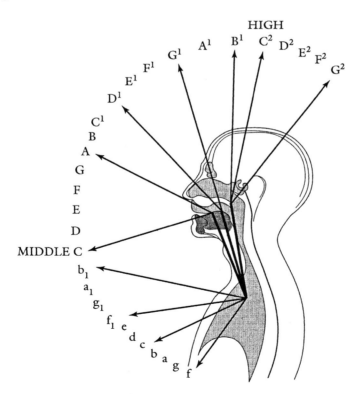

FIGURE 2–3. Change of breath direction throughout the range.

Vocal quality is produced by correct formation of vowels, while breath direction reinforces that quality through resonance. This is produced by sympathetic vibration in the throat, mouth, head, and chest cavities. Resonance amplifies the harmonic overtones in the resonant areas mentioned above. If you cup your hands over your mouth and sing into them, the sound is amplified and the quality is better. Sound echoes within your hands and creates a sympathetic vibration, or resonance, that emphasizes the beauty of the voice by producing a hi-fi system with highs and lows. Opera singers use this technique the most; rock singers the least.

VOWEL FORMATION

Various positions in the height of the tongue form all the vowels except for the sounds of *oh, aw,* and *oo* that require both tongue and lip movement.

The *ee* and *ah* series create basic tongue movement for all of the vowels in the English language. In the *ee* series, the tongue is high in the front of the mouth with the sides of the tongue touching the upper teeth while the tip touches the lower ones at the front. The highest position of the tongue raised to the upper molars is *ee*. Lowering it produces in succession *ay, eh,* and finally *agh*.

The *ah* series raises the tongue in the back of the mouth, where the highest position is *oo*. This is followed by *oh, aw*. The three latter vowels require puckering the lips. *Ah* follows in the lowest position of the tongue without puckering (unless you want a richer sound).

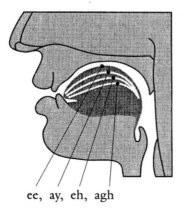
ee, ay, eh, agh

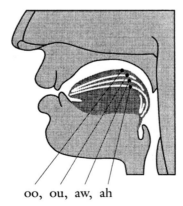
oo, ou, aw, ah

FIGURE 2–4. Tongue position for front and back vowels.

In the first example in Figure 2–4, the highest position of the tongue is in front of the mouth in the *ee* series. In the second example, the *ah* series, the tongue's highest point is in the back, beginning with *oo*. The height for each vowel is indicated with white curved lines connected to corresponding vowels.

■ ■ ■ *AH* VOWEL EXERCISE

The first vowel exercise is with *ah* as in *father*. Position the mouth, tongue, soft palate, and jaw to make *ah*, since you can *think ah* yet not *produce* a true *ah* with full quality and control.

To position *ah:*

1. Place the little finger under the third molar from the back of the upper teeth. The finger opens the voice mouth in the back, which is where the sound is produced. The finger provides space for a fuller sound and brings the center of placement into focus. Directing the breath above the finger produces the head voice, while directing it below gives the chest sound.
2. Bite *down* on the finger but *don't* bite *up* with the lower teeth.
3. Let the jaw drop loosely.
4. Direct the breath inward to fill the mouth below the finger.
5. Say *ah* in the above position.

Biting down lifts the soft palate to give upper overtones and to increase the opening at the back of the mouth for amplification.

Directing the breath below the finger and inward provides deeper resonance.

Direct the breath inward instead of wasting the breath outside the mouth. When you let air resound in the cavities of the mouth and throat, you produce resonance, or a natural amplification of the sound. Musical directors who don't know the anatomy of the voice often suggest, "Throw your voice to the back row." This is physically impossible and only results in straining. Let the sound vibrate in the mouth, and you will create resonance that projects into the auditorium.

Use a mirror while vocalising to check the positions described, since even though you are thinking the position, your muscles may not respond at first.

Summary

Bite down. Fill the back and bottom.

(Bite down on the upper molar, direct the breath inward towards the back of the mouth and fill below the finger.)

Think three *B*s: *B*ite, *B*ack, *B*ottom.

▮ ▮ ▮ *EE* VOWEL EXERCISE

In the *ee,* the front of the tongue is in a high, forward position giving a fuller chest sound and, at the same time, producing more head resonance.

1. In *ee* as in the word *eat,* the sides of the tongue touch the upper teeth while the tip contacts the lower front ones.
2. Direct the breath toward the back of mouth and under the tongue. Sound goes through muscle and bone.
3. Say *ee* in the above position.

Review the *ee* and *ah* series in Figure 2–4 for the shape of the tongue in producing *ee.*

Summary

Tongue up, fill the back and bottom.

(Fill the back and bottom of the mouth by using breath direction.)

▮ ▮ ▮ EXERCISES FOR COMBINING *AH* AND *EE*

Vocalize on the speech level

This vocalise is very important, as *ah* and *ee* form the two extreme tongue positions for all vowels in the English language.

1. Speak *ah* and *ee* as you would at your normal speaking pitch, then vocalize *ah* and *ee* on that level.

Move the tongue independently of the jaw to produce *ee* while going back and forth from *ah* to *ee*. Moving the jaw at the same time as the tongue will cause excessive tension.

As the two sounds are vocalized consecutively, they add complementary resonances to each other. The *ah* cavity allows space for a deeper resonance, while the high, forward tongue position of *ee* adds upper resonances.

The *ah* and *ee* exercise is the foundation for placement in the lower register. It also strengthens the tip of the tongue.

Summary
1. Bite down. Fill the back and bottom with the breath.
2. Tongue up in *ee.*

3

Placement for the Chest Voice

The chest voice gives depth and richness to the sound
throughout the entire range.

The chest voice is the bass part of the voice. It is the foundation of the vocal instrument. This lower voice is developed from the speech level—the pitch at which you speak. Figure 3–1 illustrates the notation in letters used in this book to identify pitches.

The lowest octave in the bass range is indicated in lowercase letters, the next octave in lowercase letters with superscript number 1, the next octave

FIGURE 3–1. Notation in letters.

from middle C up is in capital letters, the following octave is written in capital letters with superscript number 1, and the octave above the staff is in capital letters with superscript number 2.

After you practice the *ah* and *ee* exercise on the speech level, find your speaking pitch and transfer it to the piano. For soprano voices, it is around b_1, for altos around a_1 or g_1, for tenors f_1, for baritones e flat, for bass-baritones an octave below middle C. See Figure 3–1.

VOWEL FORMATION FOR THE CHEST VOICE

■ ■ ■ EXERCISES FOR THE LOWER CHEST VOICE

Vocalizing *ah* and *ee* on pitches

ah,   ee,   ah,   ee,   ah

1. Start at your speaking pitch with the positioning mentioned on pages 13–15 for *ah* and *ee* vowels. Repeat the exercise proceeding downward by half steps.
2. Stop when the voice reaches a weak level.

Keep the voice placed on the speech level position as you go lower in the range. Feel resonance opening down into the chest without pushing down or strain will occur.

Summary
1. Bite down. Fill the back and bottom with the breath.
2. Tongue up in *ee*.

The vowel circle is the basic form of vocalization for all vowels in the English language. The vowel circle most commonly used for vocalizing is *ah, ay, ee, oh, oo*, which is constructed on the *ee* and *ah* series as discussed earlier. Though the usual vowel circle is *ah, ay, ee, ou, oo*, the vowel circle used in this technique consists of the closed *ee* (as in *eat*) before the closed

Roman	Phonetic
ah	a:
ee	i:
ay	ei:
aw	ɔ:
oo	u:

FIGURE 3–2. Roman and phonetic spelling.

ay (as in *day*). This positions a higher tongue in *ay*, producing brighter overtones. The other variation of the vowel circle is the open *aw*, as in the words *law* or *jaw*, giving a fuller sound than closed *ou*.

Therefore, the vowel circle used in this book is *ah, ee, ay, aw, oo*, placing *ee* before *ay* and using the open *aw*.

Compare the two vowel circles:

1. The regular vowel circle: *ah, ay, ee, ou, oo*
2. This method's vowel circle: *ah, ee, ay, aw, oo*

Vowels are indicated by a Roman spelling; Figure 3–2 compares the Roman to phonetic spelling.

Placement for the vowel circle

Placement, or the focus of the voice, is created by positioning the mouth, tongue, soft palate, and jaw for proper formation of vowels. This positioning is necessary because most students do not sing clear vowels even if they hear them.

The following is the positioning for each individual vowel:

ah 1. Place the tip of the little finger at the upper third molar from the back and bite down on the finger; allow the lower jaw to hang loose.
    2. Direct the breath below the finger.
    3. Say *ah* (as in *father*) in this position.

ee 1. Touch the sides of the tongue against the upper teeth while the tip contacts the lower front ones.
    2. Direct the breath toward the back of the mouth below the tongue; sound vibrates through muscle and bone.

3. Say *ee* (as in *eat*) in this position.

ay 1. Keep the exact same position for *ay* as in *ee*.

    2. Say *ay* (as in *day*) in this position.

aw 1. Remove the finger and pucker the lips for the open *aw*, as if blowing a smoke ring while letting the tongue take its own position.

    2. Say *aw* (as in *law*) in this position.

oo 1. Pucker more from *aw* to *oo* allowing the sound to go further back in the mouth.

    2. Say *oo* (as in *you*) in this position.

This forms the complete vowel circle *ah, ee, ay, aw, oo* as used in this technique.

Speaking the vowel circle

1. With the above positioning, vocalize the vowel circle at your natural speaking range.

Summary

1. Bite down on upper molars for *ah*. Let the lower jaw hang loose; direct the breath below the finger.
2. Keep the tongue up for *ee* and *ay*.
3. Pucker for *aw* and *oo*, taking the finger out.

Singing the vowel circle

The vowel circle develops the lower chest voice.

ah,   ee,   ay,   aw,   oo

1. For *ah*, bite down on the upper molars; let the lower jaw hang loose while directing the breath below the finger.
2. Keep tongue up for *ee* and *ay*.
3. Pucker for *aw* and *oo*, taking the finger out.

Vocalize first on the speech level, then start on the following pitches: Sopranos on $b\flat_1$, altos on a_1 or g_1, tenors on f_1, baritones on $e\flat$, and bass-baritones on an octave below middle C. Direct the breath inward, which will provide lower abdominal support and prevent wasting the breath.

Place the hand on the upper chest to feel resonance as you let the chest reinforce the sound.

Many sing in the nose; to avoid this, hold the nose to bring the sound more into the mouth.

Alternate the little finger from one side of the mouth to the other to avoid opening on one side alone.

VOWEL FORMATION FOR REGISTRATION, STYLE, AND COLORATION

Every vowel has a different muscular formation, producing varied placements in the mouth. These contrasting vowel shapes give distinct colorations that can be used in changing sounds for different types of songs. Coloration is the tonal texture of the voice; vowels have varied textures, for example, *ee* is bright and *aw* is dark.

Because of these varied formations, vowels can also be used to change the positioning, or placement, for different registrations. *Registration* is the change in placement proceeding from the lower into the higher range or vice versa.

Each vowel creates the following textures:

1. *Ee* gives a bright quality and lifts the soft palate, providing more head resonance. *Ee* guides the voice toward the *mask* (the mask is the frontal area in the cheeks just below the eyes), producing clarity and facility in fast-spoken patter, coloratura (fast notes), or scatting.
2. *Agh* produces a brightness in the mask as well as clarity for fast patter or spoken sounds, often used in musical theater and pop music. See Exercise for the Simulated Belt Voice, page 45.
3. *Aw* provides a darker quality and forms a natural puckered position; it adds a richer sound and helps sustain held notes in the medium register.
4. *Oo* connects the head and chest. It floats the voice on the breath by releasing through the apparatus instead of holding with the placement muscles, especially in the upper register in sustaining from C^1 to G^1. See Octave Leap for *Noo* Vowel, page 52.
5. Open vowels (*ah, aw*) are for the chest voice, and closed vowels (*ee, ay,*

oo) are for the head voice. They give the correct positioning in each corresponding register.

6. Mix vowels to produce different qualities in the voice. For example, brighten an *ah* as you combine it with *ee* by forming *ee*, then sing *ah* in that position. This will be illustrated later in the exercises.

Some singers produce more resonance on one vowel than on others. Place vowels in that choice position to improve quality by shaping and feeling the sound in that preferred place; for example, darken by shaping your mouth with *oo*, then vocalize the other vowels in the *oo* position.

Summary

You can achieve voice placement by
1. Positioning the muscles of the mouth, tongue, soft palate, and jaw
2. Using different vowels

PLACEMENT FOR THE HIGH CHEST REGISTER—BELTING

The sensation in belting is similar to yelling—the difference is that belting is placed and supported; whereas yelling is screaming from the neck and strained.

The High Chest Voice in Musical Theater

In musical theater the female chest voice is brought all the way up to an octave above middle C, sometimes higher. In classical music, this is frowned upon, but in musical theater it is necessary because of style. Most music for theater is written in the weakest part of the singer's range, which is the soprano's change of voice between middle C and the octave above middle C where the chest and head have to be melded into one sound. Because most Broadway singers are not trained to do this, they resort to carrying the chest up through the head range. This belted sound is strong and exciting in this weak middle register; the mixed head sound cannot compare with the strength, aggressiveness, and clarity of the pure belted sound.

The fear in bringing chest voice up into the medium register is that it will cause nodes. When done properly, the chest voice can be produced in this range without any harm, but it must be done with technique. This book presents a classical technique that has been adapted for belting to protect the voice from the strain that can cause injury. Females have the most trouble in this register; male voices have less of a change in the registers, except for tenors.

Jerome Hines in his book *Great Singers on Great Singing* said to Marilyn Horne, "Many sopranos say they never touch the chest voice if they can help it." Miss Horne answered, "Which is crazy! They're afraid of it, because teachers don't know how to teach it. The chest voice should be taught, and sopranos should have it." In this quotation she refers to classical as well as musical theater singers; therefore, *all* singers should have a chest sound.

Many do not know whether they are in chest voice or not. One of the most effective ways to check this is to produce a strong crescendo—a crescendo is getting louder on a held note. If you are not in chest voice, the note won't have the force of the belted sound.

▮▮▮ EXERCISES FOR THE HIGH CHEST VOICE

The fifth: Pucker and lower abdomen

Vocalizing the triad of the fifth (which consists of three notes descending in thirds to the lowest note that is the fifth below the principal note) is suited to bringing chest voice into the medium register for musical theater, pop, rock, and jazz singing.

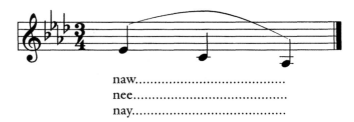

naw..
nee..
nay..

1. Pant like a dog to sense lower abdominal activity.
2. Pucker the lips, as if blowing a smoke ring, and say *naw* on the speech level.
3. For *nee* let the sides of the tongue touch the upper teeth while the tip contacts the lower front ones. In this position, pucker the lips and say *nee*. If this is difficult at first, practice on the speech level before vocalizing on pitches.

4. Keep the same position of *nee* for *nay,* producing more brilliance to the sound.
5. After the above is mastered, connect with breath support by pulling the lower abdomen in on each top note. See next exercise.

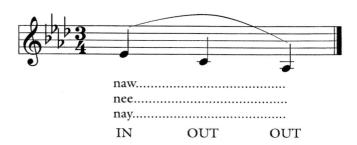

naw..
nee..
nay..

IN   OUT   OUT

The fifth with abdominal support

1. On *nay* pull abdomen in on all three notes to support the end of the phrase. Keep the chest up while pulling the lower abdomen in. Tighten buttocks and legs to support the sound, but don't compress the chest.
2. When you reach A♭ (six notes above middle C), change the vowel to *nah* instead of *naw,* which will form a more horizontal opening with a slight pucker. Lower voices change a step lower.

Use the mixed head voice as a guide to produce a brighter chest quality, if the chest is too heavy or tight. Sing in the mixed head voice first, then place the chest voice there, hearing and imagining it before singing. See Chapter 6 on Placement for the Middle Register in the Legitimate or Classical Voice.

Proceed up the scale in half steps until the top note reaches the limit of your chest range, which can be felt when you begin to strain for the note.

As you descend the fifth in thirds, ride the breath down the front of the face.

Summary
1. Pucker
2. Lower abdomen: In, out, out.

Octave drop

Instead of the pucker-abdomen vertical position, an alternate technique is a horizontal opening of the mouth.

yah.......................
yee.......................
yay.......................
yaw.......................
yoo.......................

1. Bite down on the tip of the little finger at the third upper molar from the back while dropping the lower jaw.
2. Attack from above, as if dropping down on the note.
3. Direct breath below the finger for the bottom note.
4. Follow vowel formation as mentioned in the vowel circle.
5. Breathe after each vowel.

The *y* before each vowel lifts the soft palate for upper resonances.

Bite down from above for proper preparation on the attack so as not to reach for the note. See page 25 on The Attack.

This exercise produces a brighter sound than the pucker-abdomen exercise.

As before, if the chest sound is too heavy or tight, lighten the sound by first singing in the head, then put the chest in the head voice place. See the Legitimate Sound in the Middle Range, page 36.

Summary
1. Bite down from above; drop the jaw.
2. Follow vowel circle position.
3. Pull lower abdomen in on top note.

BREATH DIRECTION ASCENDING
AND DESCENDING THE SCALE

Breath direction aids in retaining voice placement. When ascending and descending the range, placement changes gradually. Control this by feeling the breath ride up the back of the head ascending and ride down the front of the face descending.

THE ATTACK

The *attack* is the physical formation of a note—the positioning for placement—before actually singing it: It is the preparation for the note. Anticipate the positioning for placement before the attack; otherwise the sound may be flat even if you prehear the pitch, or the voice may crack.

For the attack, imagine the positioning of the mouth, jaw, tongue, and soft palate before the sound and do not scoop to the note. Scooping is when the note is approached from below the pitch and is a sign of an untrained voice. Attack the note from above to avoid reaching.

Lift the soft palate on the attack to place the voice in the upper part of the sound or in the mushroom, as described in Figure 2–2 on page 10. Also see the section below for a description of lifting the soft palate. Once you have acquired the positioning, extend that positioning through sense memory beyond the apparatus, especially in the upper register.

FOUR WAYS TO LIFT THE SOFT PALATE
1. Feel a biting down motion on the molars with the little finger at the third top molar while letting the jaw hang loosely.
2. Precede each vowel with *y* by saying *ee* before each vowel.
3. Pucker the lips as if blowing a smoke ring.
4. Yawn. The beginning of a yawn locates the soft palate. As the yawn progresses, the tongue is tightened. So feel only the beginning of the yawn.

The choice of any of the above suggestions in lifting the palate is determined by register. In this book the choice will be made for you in each specific exercise. Begin the attack with an inner thought of the position before breathing. Thinking this position alerts the shape of the muscles, allowing the sounding of the note to pass freely. This is what is meant by anticipating the attack—just as a runner gets into position for the start of the race. The whole apparatus is set to go into action.

Once you know the proper position for each vowel and note, all coordination is regulated by the ear, which is hearing the selected pitch, quality, and intensity. This procedure seems very involved at first but will soon become a semiconscious reflex.

4

How to Practice

You get out whatever you put in.

℘

Singing is like any physical skill. The brain, nervous system, and physical toning has to be developed. The amount of practice you put in will determine how accomplished you will be. Know what you want technically in your practice. Each exercise covers a different technique. Choose them individually according to your needs. Don't just go through the motions of vocalizing; schedule a regular time every day. The more time that you put in, the quicker you will advance.

PROGRAMMING YOUR PRACTICE

In the beginning, plan your practice so as not to strain your voice. Time yourself and take rests between each exercise, otherwise you may make yourself hoarse. Getting started with a method can cause exertion and it may take some time until you learn the proper production. Resting between each exercise helps you monitor your voice. Then you will have a better idea of when to stop rather than singing for an hour without resting and having no voice left.

At first, practice for just a half hour a day, dividing the time into two segments:

FIRST FIFTEEN MINUTES
1. breathing exercise
2. vowel circle
3. the fifth—chest voice

SECOND FIFTEEN MINUTES

1. head voice scale of the fifth (See Exercises for the Legitimate Head Voice in the Middle Range, page 37).
2. vocalize song on one vowel.

Use the vowel *ah* with *n;* as you pucker, it becomes *naw.*

WARMING UP

If you don't practice for a day or two, you will feel the difference in a lack of response physically as in any other muscular activity, like dancing or jogging. You will feel out of shape. Consistent practice tones muscles and coordinates the brain, ear, and vocal apparatus.

Different kinds of singing call for different types of warming up. Doing folk music or light pop music doesn't take as much warming up as opera or a very high belt.

LEARNING A SONG

Learn the notes of a song first, instead of singing it with the lyrics immediately. It is vital to find the proper vocal placement for the notes before adding the words. If you don't find the placement first, there is a tendency to reach for high notes, close off on consonants, and tighten the vocal apparatus. By the time you are ready to sing the song, a multitude of improper tensions will have been incorporated into your experience.

Learn the music separately, then vocalize the song on a single vowel to find the placement.

∎∎∎ EXERCISE FOR LEARNING A SONG

1. Read through the lyrics to find the meaning of the words.
2. Learn the melody by listening to the recording or playing it on an instrument without singing.

The best way to learn a melody is to have an accompanist record it on a cassette tape, playing the melody and accompaniment. This applies even to jazz pieces where the melody is not played—so that the singer can change the rhythms. Have the accompanist record the accompaniment once with the melody and once without. When you know the song, you can change rhythms to follow the jazz style.

Chapter Four

Applying vocalization to a song

1. Vocalize the song on a vowel, placing the voice and bringing in lower abdominal support. Choose the proper vowel according to registers listed below:
   a. chest voice belt on *yah*
   b. head voice mix on *naw*
   c. high register from A♭ above the staff on *nay* or *ee*
2. Vocalize the melody with the lyrics in the vowel placement position.

A lot of students learn music by listening to the singer on an original cast album. This can be a disadvantage because the singer's voice may be different from yours, making you think that you have to imitate the sound. Listen once for general quality and style, but keep your own individuality that is closest to the character played.

After you have learned the song vocally, find the scene in the song through a basic acting technique that is discovering the objective and obstacle in the scene. This will be covered later under acting techniques.

PSYCHO-CYBERNETICS, OR VISUALIZATION

The most effective way of practicing is to use the technique of *psycho-cybernetics,* or visualization, discovered by Dr. Maxwell Maltz.

Dr. Maltz says, "Experimental and clinical psychologists have proved beyond a shadow of a doubt that the human nervous system cannot tell the difference between an 'actual' experience and an experience imagined vividly and in detail. When you 'experience,' something happens inside your nervous system and your midbrain. New 'engrams' and 'neural' patterns are recorded in the gray matter of your brain."

Following this premise Dr. Maltz suggests imagining the complete experience before executing it. Sense every detail in singing, by hearing the pitch, quality, and dynamics and feeling the actual physical production of the notes. The brain and nervous system register this imagined experience, so you have practiced the steps already, making the correct response more immediate when you sing. It is not only more efficient; it also saves the voice from tiring and avoids a lot of bad habits by bringing together details you miss when you sing right away. This technique is particularly effective when you are ill and cannot use your voice, but must review the material. Psycho-cybernetics can be applied to every aspect of learning, such as

- vocalizing
- learning a song
- incorporating the scene in a song
- rehearsing whole concerts or acts

INHIBITIONS

Many students are shy about vocalizing with roommates or neighbors within hearing distance. Find a place that is the least disturbing to others. Practice when they're out, if possible. If not, practice within reasonable hours. Don't feel guilty. Realize it is your need and privilege to practice. Your advancement will depend on how much time you put in. With others around, you may feel self-conscious for the first five minutes, but you will soon forget that they are there later.

5

The Range

The larger the range, the fuller the repertoire
you will be able to sing.

𝄞

Before extending the voice into the higher range, we need to define range and explain how it varies in different voices.

Range encompasses the highest to lowest notes of a voice. Classification is not by range alone but by vocal timbre, or quality (richness, size, or weight) of the sound.

VOCAL CLASSIFICATION

Classical music categories are

FEMALE VOICES	MALE VOICES	
coloratura soprano	countertenor	bass-baritone buffo
lyric soprano	lyric tenor	bass
dramatic soprano	Heldentenor	
mezzo-soprano	lyric baritone	
contralto	Verdi baritone	

Musical theater and pop music categories are

FEMALE VOICES	MALE VOICES
soprano	tenor
alto-belt/mezzo	baritone
	bass

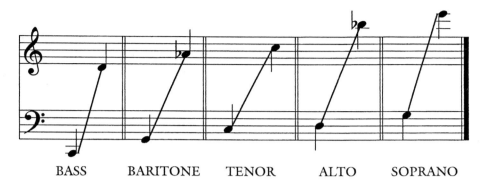

BASS   BARITONE   TENOR   ALTO   SOPRANO

FIGURE 5–1. Ranges in specific types of voices.

(The term *mezzo* is often used in the role breakdown in ads for auditions; this is a misnomer as it usually means sopranos who belt in the chest voice.)

Figure 5–1 shows ranges in specific types of voices.

Voices are classified by quality and weight of sound—lightness or darkness—and not by range alone.

Most opera voices cover a minimum of three octaves; many voices extend even further. Pop and jazz singers often have an octave-and-a-half range but extend into another octave or more in the falsetto range for riffing or scatting.

Do not push for an increase in range in either direction, but let the voice expand gradually without straining—this is a matter of muscles stretching with practice. Being at perfect ease with singing a certain high or low note, you can certainly sing a half-step higher or lower without straining. Let the comfort of your instrument and sound guide you. Most important, don't reach for high notes and don't push down for low notes, as pushing or reaching will shut the throat off.

6

Placement for the Middle Register in the Legitimate or Classical Voice

A mixture of head and chest voice is used
in the middle register.
Head voice is the treble in a stereo, and chest is the bass.

℘

The greatest challenge in the vocal range is in the middle voice where most singing takes place. A fine tuning of the proper mixture between the head voice and the chest voice is needed especially at the change in registers.

CHANGE IN REGISTERS

The three registers in the voice are low, middle, and high. Proceeding from the lower range into the middle, the chest voice switches over into the head voice because of the physical limitations of the vocal apparatus. The vocal apparatus consists of two primary muscles, the cryco-thyroid muscle and the interarytenoid muscle, which work in synergy by pulling against and balancing each other. Passing from one register into another, muscles need a fine adjustment of positioning to proceed into the next register, similar to changing gears in a car. This change is called *registration,* or the lower-upper passaggio areas. The change in registers for sopranos are from

- chest voice to the middle register at E in the lower passaggio
- middle to the high voice at E¹, in the upper passaggio

Altos change a whole step lower, tenors an octave lower, baritones an octave and a whole step lower, while basses change an octave and a major third lower.

If you don't shift gears to mix the head with the chest, your voice may crack or even stop sounding—this is called the break in the voice; see Figure 6–1. When you mix the head voice with the chest at the change, it becomes the legitimate, or legit, voice. A mixed head voice is produced by filling the upper and lower cavities of the mouth with the sound (see Figure 2–2).

MELDING THE CHEST VOICE
WITH THE HEAD VOICE

In classical and legitimate Broadway singing, this blending of the registers produces an even coloration throughout the range for a seamless voice, or a voice without changes in registers. This is the aim in all beautiful singing.

When the pure chest sound is brought up very high, the change in registration becomes very pronounced, sounding as two different voices— full chest and light head voice. Bernadette Peters' singing is an obvious example of this.

Meld from one register into another by blending tone coloration. Tone color is controlled by how much chest or head voice is used. As you proceed from the chest voice into head voice, lighten the chest sound by having more mushroom (see Figure 2–2); and when going down into the chest voice, darken the head voice by directing the breath below the center of placement.

THE BREAK IN THE VOICE

As mentioned, if the differences become too great, not only is the sound like two different voices, but you can also have a hole in the voice where the sound will shut off; this is called the *break* in the voice, most common in sopranos and tenors.

Correct this break by using a classical head and chest mix through the change of voice in lyric ballads. When the section is aggressive, as in uptunes—fast songs—or dramatic ballads, use the pure chest sound.

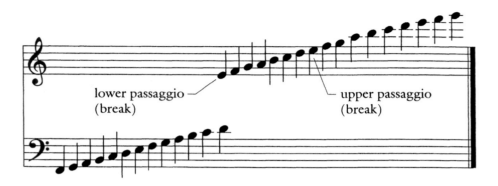

FIGURE 6–1. Change in registers or break in the voice.

For climactic and aggressive phrases, stay in the chest voice as long as possible, then change over into the forward head voice sound. See the Simulated Belt Voice, page 45. When the vibrato is taken out and the voice placed in the mask, the head voice can sound like it is belted. Control the vibrato by driving the breath toward the mask directly from the lower abdomen.

Know exactly where to change into head; ask your voice teacher, or if you don't have an instructor, an obvious guide is to change into the head when feeling strained.

Many singers, especially sopranos, have problems in melding the upper and lower registers. Retaining the upper part of the sound—the mushroom—melds the registers throughout the range.

To join registers, imagine the legitimate positioning when singing in the chest. This connects the placement and support for the chest voice to enter the head voice. Glide up the back of the mouth with the breath through the mushroom as you proceed into the head voice. In the high belt range, think of the mushroom extending beyond the mouth on the breath to avoid constriction. When you sing on the breath, you feel the breath passing through the throat and mouth without being held by the vocal muscles.

LEGITIMATE HEAD VOICE MIX

To get into the head voice sound, throw your voice as high as you can on an *oo,* pretending you're an opera singer. Some singers are afraid of sounding operatic; however, this exercise will give the sensation of a fully placed and supported head voice. It takes a long time to acquire a real opera sound, so don't worry about sounding operatic. Simulate the opera soprano by keeping the breath in the mouth and pushing from your lower abdomen as you throw the *oo* into the head. Throwing the *oo* vowel into the head voice narrows the vocal tract like a tube and mixes the head voice and the chest voice automatically. The legitimate voice is typical in music of Rodgers and Hammerstein and of Lerner and Loewe.

▮▮▮ MELDING THE HEAD VOICE WITH THE CHEST VOICE

On the speech level

1. Lift the soft palate with a full intake of breath, then sigh on the syllable *ha* on the speech level. Ride the breath down the front of the face and as you reach the chest voice, slightly release the breath pressure, then you won't feel a change going into the chest range. Sliding down is the guide to melding the head into the chest; musically this is called *portamento.*

Melding in singing

1. Sing The Octave Fall Exercise with that same gliding down the front of the face on the mushroom.

Be sure to release the breath pressure slightly before entering the chest voice.

This exercise requires a good deal of patience in floating on the breath instead of manipulating the muscles.

THE PASSAGGIO, OR CHANGE IN THE UPPER VOICE

In the passaggio, registration shifts from the middle into the high register. Placement for this change is the pucker–abdomen position. Puckering the lips narrows the vocal tract, connecting the lower abdominal support with the upper vocal apparatus. Some schools call this *covering* the voice.

When you reach this upper break at E^1, throw the breath slightly beyond the head to avoid holding with the throat (see Figure 2–3 on The Change of Breath Direction Throughout the Range). In the five note scale (see page 37) start with the pucker position for *ee* and open into a slight horizontal position on the top note for a bright *ah;* after starting the note horizontally, adjust into a pucker. The brighter opening with the *ah* gives the ring in the mask, and the pucker connects the sound with the lower abdominal support. Follow the breath and allow your ear and comfort to direct the change.

Make the *ee* vowel in the passaggio with a natural *oo* pucker instead of spreading the lips. Otherwise, you can feel as if you're choking. Pavarotti calls this "Strangoolation!"

When you crescendo at this transition point (E^1), increase the volume through the mushroom. Increasing the volume through only the lower part of the sound can shut off the throat.

Because these exercises are mechanical, they must be practiced carefully, particularly in this range. All formations and manipulations should be done with relative ease in order not to strain. The final control is guided by the ear and the comfort of the sound. It helps to hear the pitches and vocal quality ahead instead of making them with the throat.

THE LEGITIMATE SOUND IN THE MIDDLE RANGE

As mentioned, the legitimate sound in the middle range is a mixture of the chest voice and the head voice. The head voice alone in females is called a falsetto; it needs to be mixed with the chest voice to become head voice.

Exercises for the middle head voice for sopranos can begin on F, for altos on E♭, tenors on f_1, baritones on e♭ and basses on c or a.

Middle head voice exercises can be taken up to G^1 for sopranos, F^1 for altos, G for tenors, F for baritones and D for basses. Beyond this range the voice goes into a change of placement for the high voice (see Chapter 9).

▎▎▎ EXERCISES FOR THE LEGITIMATE HEAD VOICE IN THE MIDDLE RANGE

Three note scale

The three note scale is a simple exercise for mixed head voice in the middle register and is excellent for a *legato,* or smooth, line.

hm nee........................ naw..

1. For *nee,* pucker the lips, as if blowing a smoke ring, while touching the sides of the tongue against the upper teeth and the tip against the lower. You may find this hard to coordinate, so practice in the mirror on the speech level before singing it.

2. Place *nee* in the mask by preceding it with *hm.*

3. Retain the same pucker for *naw.* The tongue will automatically take its own position but imagine the tongue high as in *nee.*

Summary
1. Pucker with tongue up for *ee.*
2. Use same position for *aw.*

Five note scale

The five note scale on *nee* and *nah* extends the mixed head voice into the middle and upper range. Puckering gives a rich vibrato and is used to sustain a dark, warm sound. It also adds body and color to a light, nasal voice.

hm nee...............................nah...

1. For *nee,* pucker your lips, as if blowing a smoke ring, touching the sides of the tongue against the upper teeth while the tip contacts the lower ones.
2. Place *nee* in the mask (cheeks) by preceding it with *hm.*
3. Retain the same pucker for the *nah,* keeping the tongue high as in *nee. Nah* sounds like *naw* with the pucker.

Puckering the lips narrows the vocal tract connecting the chest and head voice with the breath. *Ee* raises the soft palate, adding upper resonances to the sound.

For the five note scale, sopranos can start on F, altos on E♭, tenors on f_1, baritones on $e♭_1$, and basses an octave below middle C.

Summary
1. Pucker with tongue up for *ee*
2. Same position for *ah*

Breath support for the five note scale

Once proper formation of the pucker and tongue position is achieved, you can coordinate it with abdominal support.

1. Leave the lower abdomen out on the attack, then pull the lower abdomen in while ascending the scale.

This projects the breath up and out to the high note, crescendoing and supporting the sound with the lower abdomen.

hm nee....................................nah..

Summary
1. Pucker.
2. Lower abdomen—out, in, out, in.

Scale of thirds

The scale of thirds is an alternate exercise for the head voice that goes back and forth from *ee* to *ah*. *Ee* gives a high tongue placement for *ah*, adding a ring or upper resonance to *ah*.

hmnee,ah,ee,ah,ee,ah,ee,ah,ee   nee,ah,ee,ah,ee,ah,ee,ah,ee

1. For *nee,* pucker the lips, touching the sides of the tongue against the upper teeth while the tip contacts the lower ones.
2. Precede *nee* with *hm,* placing it in the mask.
3. Retain the same pucker for *nah,* imagining the high tongue as in *nee.*
4. Use the tongue *independently* of the jaw in proceeding back and forth from both vowels. Don't let the jaw go up and down in changing from *ee* to *ah.*

   Descending the scale, keep the high palate position from *ee* to *ah.*

Summary
1. Pucker for *nee* and *nah.* Retain the *nee* puckered position for both vowels.
2. Use the tongue, changing from *nee* to *nah.*

   The *ah* will have a slight *aw* sound with the pucker.

RESONANCE: THE SPECTRUM OF SOUND IN SINGING

The amount of resonance used determines the categorization of voices. The degree of resonance and vibrato used determines the quality of sound. When the voice is placed and supported properly, all the resonators—cavities in the throat, mouth, head, and chest—amplify the sound-producing resonance. Vocal vibrato is a natural, even oscillation above and below the main pitch that gives the voice vitality, buoyancy, and richness. Amplification of resonance can be increased by imagining the sound being reinforced by the cavities of the head down to the chest, bringing in sympathetic vibration from the head and the chest. Imagine a vocal spectrum with the opera singer at one end and the soft rock singer at the other. The opera sound is the fullest and most lush in size and quality, and the soft rock singer is the light, breathy sound at the other end of the spectrum. If you think operatic, you will automatically make a fuller sound because the opera sound is supported and vibrates with resonance.

Degrees of Resonance

Different styles of singing require varying degrees of resonance.

1. *Opera* resonates fully throughout the range. Even soft passages need to resonate with a height and depth of sound.
2. *Light opera* vibrates throughout, but the quality has less upper and lower overtones than opera.
3. *Legitimate musical theater* resounds more frontally with less overtones than light opera.
4. *Jazz* resonates in chest passages with a spoken sound; but the head voice, as in scatting, has to be straight (without vibrato).
5. *Pop* uses a breathy, spoken sound in the lower register, resonating in climaxes.
6. *Hard rock* has a breathy, spoken sound in the chest register and a driven breath pressure toward the nose in the upper register that often approximates yelling.

It is important to know how to control resonance, or lack of it, since it produces the kind of voice you use.

In the Broadway belt style, musical theater uses a predominance of pure chest voice with resonance. In the upper register a straighter sound (with less vibrato) toward the mask is used.

Barbara Cooke, in her Broadway years, was an ideal example of a legitimate soprano with a beautiful upper and lower resonance. The perfect male voice was John Raitt, with a full resonant sound without being operatic.

Controlling Resonance

The *noo* exercise, see page 52, is favorable for controlling vibrato in pop, rock, and jazz. Breath direction in the *noo* exercise can be changed to eliminate vibrato by using a steady driven breath pressure from the abdomen toward the nose, producing the straight voice. The best exponent of this is Barbra Streisand in her rock singing.

When you release the breath in the *noo* exercise, filling all the cavities, you achieve a legitimate sound with a vibrant, rich quality. The more you bring the breath down into the mouth and back toward the soft palate, the sound changes into a classical voice with full vibrato.

7

The Mask Technique for the Middle Register

The mask gives the ring, or brightness, to the sound;
it provides brilliance and carrying power to the voice.

♭♪

The mask technique is another method used in the mixed head voice that is produced by spreading the lips and directing the breath from the lower abdomen to the cheek area below the eyes. A typical suggestion for the mask is "Sing high under the eyes." Although breath direction is high under the eyes, the breath does not go into the sinuses enough to affect the sound in projection. Directing the breath toward the mask, however, positions the larynx to give the ring in the voice. This ring creates brightness, or upper overtones, in the quality. Use *Ee* to achieve ring in the voice because of its high overtones; this ringing sensation gives brilliance and carrying power.

Many teachers teach only one method. The German Technique uses the pucker, whereas the Italian Technique emphasizes the mask. One tends to be the opposite from the other. This book combines three techniques: the German Technique, the Italian Technique, and the Chewing Method. The different techniques are used for specific effects. For instance, puckering rounds and enriches the sound, while the mask produces brilliance and agility in coloratura (rapid notes). The mask also gives clarity to fast patter—rapid singing of words. In diction, if the sound is too dark and heavy it becomes muffled and unwieldy. This is the main reason opera singers' diction is often not understood—the sound is too heavy and dark, like an elephant trying to fly through the trees. Finally, the chewing technique places the voice in the mouth and relieves tension.

Be open about trying various approaches. Don't be afraid to combine them. I remember when I was a student and my teacher suggested that I use the pucker in the upper change of voice—the passaggio. Depending only on the mask technique, I did it very hesitantly, and consequently it didn't work. If I had been more open-minded, I would have avoided many years of uncomfortable singing through the break in the voice.

The mask works well up to D^1 then tends to cut off through the passaggio, which is the upper change in the voice around E^1, at which point the pucker-abdomen exercise is preferred.

Voices too dark, dull, or throaty need the ring in the mask that can be achieved by the following techniques:

1. Hum in the cheeks and place the vowel in a horizontal aperture in the humming place.
2. Combine the pucker technique with breath direction toward the mask to achieve more ring.
3. Precede each vowel with *y* (*ee* sound) = *y-a, y-ee*.

All the suggestions above are applied later in specific vocal exercises.

BREATH DIRECTION TECHNIQUE

The breath in the mask technique is directed into *both* cheeks, high under the eyes.

Musical theater placement is more forward in the mask than opera is. This is important for diction; many times the words are just as important as the sound, and in some instances more crucial. The opera sound, resonating in the back as well as toward the mask, has more opulence than the more frontal Broadway sound.

The mask changes breath direction in different registers. You control the sound by where you direct your breath. As you go up the range, direct the breath up the back of the head when ascending and down the front of the face when descending. Enlarge this breath direction by expanding beyond the head and below the chest in the higher range to free the voice and extend the sound. This expansion is an image (see Figure 2–3). Releasing the breath through the muscles instead of holding, especially in high notes, prevents constriction and shrillness. As you proceed throughout the range, retain the mushroom to enable the muscles to connect into the next register.

THE RING

To produce the ring:

1. Feel the ringing sensation in the LOWER REGISTER by biting down on the finger; the breath is directed under the finger into the back part of the mouth. Let the jaw hang loosely as biting up will tighten the jaw and inhibit sound.
2. Direct the breath in the MIDDLE REGISTER toward the upper part of the cheeks from the abdomen.
3. Throw the breath beyond the head into the HIGH REGISTER at F^1, expanding the mask image. This breath direction is the same in the pucker-abdomen technique.

THE LEGITIMATE VOICE

The mask technique gives more ring but has less bottom than the pucker-abdomen exercise. The mask technique is preferable to some who choose not to pucker the lips. It makes the voice sound brighter and more youthful while adding clarity to fast patter. The pucker, however, gives a fuller, darker sound that is advantageous for a sustaining, dramatic quality or a more mature sound.

▮▮▮ EXERCISE FOR THE LEGITIMATE VOICE

Descending fifth

The Descending Fifth is a popular exercise for vocalizing the mask voice.

nyaghm, nyaghm, nyaghm, nyaghm, nyaghm

1. Vocalize *nyaghm, nyaghm* (pronounced *nee-aghm* as in *hat*— the *gh* is silent) on the speech level. Direct the breath from the lower abdomen to the cheeks while also resonating in the mouth.
2. Vocalize the *nyaghm, nyaghm,* singing the descending fifth scale.

Female high voices can start on C^1, as shown above, lower voices start one whole step lower. Tenors begin an octave lower, baritones an octave and a whole step lower, and basses an octave and a third lower.

For support, pull in lower abdomen on the top note for the attack and continue to pull in while descending to the lower note.

After doing the descending fifth, do any of the middle voice exercises in the mask place: the Third, Scale of the Fifth, or Scale of Thirds.

Summary
1. Ring in the mask.
2. Support with the lower abdomen.

THE SIMULATED BELT VOICE

Use the mask technique in the head voice to simulate a belted sound in the upper register if you cannot belt up too high.

▮▮▮ EXERCISE FOR THE SIMULATED BELT VOICE

Place the voice in the mask, driving the breath forward toward the cheeks from the lower abdomen to eliminate any vibrato.

nyaghm,   nyaghm,   nyaghm,   nyaghm,   nyaghm

1. Place the voice in the mask, saying, *"Agh!"* (as in *hat*) very aggressively on the speech level, similar to attacking someone verbally, for example "Agh, go away!"

2. Vocalize the Descending Fifth in this placement.

3. For the attack, pull the lower abdomen in on the first note.

This is a very strenuous exercise, so rest between each try; close your mouth, swallow, and chew a little to relax the vocal muscles.

Aim the breath toward the cheeks instead of the nose, or you will be too nasal. The feeling is like exclaiming instead of singing.

VOCAL QUALITY IN MUSICAL THEATER

Adapt the coloration of your voice to whatever the composer demands; musical theater today prefers a forward mask sound, reserving the legitimate sound for specific songs or important climactic phrases. Use the *nyaghm* mask technique principally for this forward placement, cutting down the resonance of the legitimate sound and bringing a clarity to the diction.

On Broadway, it is preferred that the singer be more dramatic than too vocal. The opera sound is good for building the voice and for attaining the fullest and most beautiful sound you can make for climaxes. Oftentimes, they put the big opera voice in the chorus for extended range and climactic numbers.

PART TWO

Intermediate Technique

8

Techniques for Projection

Projection is voice, diction, and action.

℘

After achieving placement and support of the voice, you can develop techniques for projection that are (1) amplifying the voice physically, (2) enunciating words, and (3) singing on the breath.

MECHANICAL PROJECTION

Projection is carrying power in the voice. The most common misconception about it is that you must project the breath out of the mouth. The advice "Throw your voice to the back row" is physically impossible. The physical aspect of extending the voice starts with air passing through the vocal folds initiating the sound; then the resonating cavities of the throat, mouth, head, and chest amplify the quality of the sound; and finally, air pressure controls the volume: The combination of all three projects the voice physically.

To achieve this, direct your breath inward to fill all cavities of the throat, mouth, and pharynx, producing sympathetic vibration or resonance. You can feel a ringing in the mask at the sinuses, and vibration in the chest, through sympathetic vibration or bone conduction.

In projecting, let the resonance, or ring, take over the carrying power and increase volume by breath pressure only when a fuller sound is necessary. This singing on resonance keeps the voice from straining.

PROJECTION PLUS INTENTION

Complete voice projection consists of three elements:

1. Voice production that includes placement and support
2. Diction that deals with clarity of vowels and consonants
3. Action that projects the sound through intention

Use these three elements rather than physical production alone, or the voice will sound mechanically projected. Note in the exclamation "I've told you a *mil*lion times. *When* are you going to do it?!!!" you accented the stressed syllables on the vowels *i* and *e* while using an acting action such as, pounding it in, with the initial consonants *m* and *wh*. This gives an expressive projection as compared to a purely mechanical one where volume alone is raised. Thus, true projection consists of the combination of voice, diction, and action.

DICTION

To delve into the intricacies of diction would take much more space than we have in this little book. Once you have a thorough grasp of diction, however, there are definite rhythmic techniques used in singing for enunciation.

Let the idea of what you are saying be your guide rather than the multitude of syllables. When you think of the idea it will help you go to the stressed syllable while letting other syllables be unstressed, thus creating *speech melody*. This is shown in *My Fair Lady* where Professor Higgins teaches Liza Doolittle speech melody by playing different pitched drums to hear the accents in the rise and fall of speech melody.

In fast patter when you over enunciate the many syllables, it is like the immigrant just off the boat who emphasizes every syllable. The meaning is lost because you hear all of the syllables instead of just the stressed ones. Also, classical singers are often not understood because they give equal stress to all notes for a beautiful line, retaining the purity of vowels on each syllable. Speech melody can be maintained by simply not accenting the unstressed vowels.

The next step in diction is to anticipate the initial consonant before the stressed syllable. Do this by stealing time from the previous note, then form and sound the consonant before the downbeat of the stressed word. For

the.........*mm*m an   I............*lll* ove.

FIGURE 8–1. Anticipating the consonants.

example, in the song "The Man I Love," the *m* would go on the previous note "The"—"The...mmman," and the "l" on the previous "I"—"I...lllove." Precede with the consonant on the previous beat, then sound the consonant on the actual beat of the word itself. (See Figure 8–1.) The duration of the consonants, not the force, projects clarity.

I remember as a voice student at Juilliard I studied under a very famous speech teacher and was determined to have excellent diction. The harder I worked, the less I was understood. It wasn't until years later when, as an actor studying Speech in Poetry with Ms. Alice Hermes at Berghof Studios, I learned speech melody—the stressed and unstressed syllables and the technique of preceding with the consonants with duration (not force)— then the whole picture of diction fell into place.

Later, Ms. Hermes, who was the head of the Speech Department, invited me to join the staff at Berghof Studios. I taught Voice and Acting in Singing for more than thirty years, while I also had my private voice studio at the same time.

In music, many unstressed syllables are written with the same rhythmic value as stressed syllables. It is necessary to keep the unstressed syllables lighter than the stressed, especially in a *legato* or sustained line. Speak the lyrics first to feel the natural flow of the speech melody, then accent and anticipate the consonants in the words accordingly.

In pop music, the singer is supposed to change the rhythms so that unstressed syllables will be shorter, as in speaking. This is indicative of the pop style; and if you don't do so, you are considered square.

When you are singing in fast patter, it is important to place the words in the mask position to give the voice frontal ring for brightness and clarity. If you use a heavy, dark quality, the words become muffled in all the vibrato, or overtones.

Summary

1. Diction has mainly to do with the idea of what you are saying that produces speech melody with stressed and unstressed syllables.
2. Anticipate initial consonants on important syllables.
3. Use the mask placement especially in fast patter.

SINGING ON THE BREATH

When you first learn to sing, it is necessary to work on the mechanical aspects of setting up and using the singing apparatus properly. As you master the physical positioning of the mouth, tongue, soft palate, and jaw, the quality of sound becomes richer and larger so that you can include hearing that vocal quality in the sound before the attack. In the preparation of your attack, you cannot anticipate hearing the fuller quality until it has been developed to some degree. Another singer's sound can be imitated, which often is beneficial in exploring sounds, but eventually the aim is to prehear your own quality.

At first, hear only the pitch and vowel before making the sound; later, when the voice develops, add quality and phrasing.

Couple this prehearing of sound with breath direction, which controls and reinforces the sound. Directing the breath in the nose produces a nasal sound; directing it in the back of the mouth produces a deeper and darker sound. The vocal positioning or placement has to be in focus before you can effectively amplify it with breath direction.

Finally, in advanced singing, sound is ultimately controlled by this prehearing and breath direction that prepares the physical production of the note. When this prehearing and breath direction is released through the throat and mouth instead of being held by the apparatus, it gives the sensation of singing on the breath.

▌▌▌ EXERCISES FOR SINGING ON THE BREATH

Octave leap for *noo* vowel

The *oo* vowel produces a natural singing on the breath. The puckered position narrows the vocal tract into a tubular shape, allowing you to feel the breath above and below the larynx. In this way the *oo* in the legitimate voice automatically connects the chest sound with the head voice that is called the head voice mix.

There is a floating, soaring quality that releases into high and low resonances automatically when singing on the breath. Pure mechanical manipulation cannot achieve this: The voice is best produced reflexively with prehearing and feeling the sound. Mechanical manipulation also causes excessive tension, restricting overtones.

Use the *noo* vowel exercise for sustaining long notes, especially in the passaggio for the change from middle to the high voice. This change is at E^1 for sopranos, a whole step lower for mezzos, an octave lower for tenors, an octave and a whole step lower for baritones, and an octave and a third lower for basses. The *oo* position in this range for the passaggio is called *covering*.

The tubular shape, through a natural pucker, gives a height and depth to the voice. This provides a two-way stretch that not only produces beauty in the sound but also helps the singer stay on pitch through overtones. When done correctly, the tone floats effortlessly on the breath, in the center of the sound. The only effort is a slight pulling in of the lower abdomen.

The following *noo* vowel exercise allows a smooth connection between lower and upper register and blends the coloration of the voice between chest and head registers.

noo,   noo,   noo

1. Say *oo* on the speech level in the mouth. The *oo* has a natural pucker; don't force the position. The position of the lower chest note on *noo* needs to have the mushroom above the upper teeth.

2. As you feel the height and depth of *oo* on the speech level, sing by throwing the breath from the chest into the upper head voice, staying in the same place as the bottom note. Repeat *noo* on the upper note.

You can imitate an operatic soprano on the speech level to get the feeling of the head voice sound. This connects you with the legitimate singing sound that is a mixture of head and chest voice.

Start on middle C for female voices and an octave lower for male voices. Lower voices start a second or third lower according to your category. For higher voices, use the lower chest note up to E; then continuing above E, sing in the mixed head voice. For lower voices, use the mixed head voice according to your corresponding change in voice.

Make the lower note short and release the breath quickly into the upper note. Release on the breath saying the *noo* versus making *noo* with the mouth. Proceeding into the upper octave, feel a two-way stretch with the breath. This assists in mixing the head with the chest. Lifting the placement will lose the chest part of the sound. In sustaining follow the breath out instead of forcing it.

Summary
1. Mushroom on lower note.
2. Release in the same place on the breath with a two-way stretch.

Octave leap with turn

Once this first step of the *noo* vowel exercise is conquered, add a turn on the upper octave with an *ee*.

noo,   noo,   ee...............................

1. *Ee* should be placed with a slight pucker of *noo,* giving *ee* a floating release on the breath into mushroom.

   This mushroom on the turn of *ee* with a pucker is vital for sustaining and crescendoing in the upper range. It also gives an upper ring to the sound. As you sustain the note, expand up into the mushroom; and don't pull down too much, or it can shut the sound off.

Summary
1. Mushroom.
2. Release in the same place as the lower note.
3. Release *ee* in the *oo* place.

TECHNIQUE FOR TONAL CONTROL

▮▮▮ MESSA DI VOCE

Messa di voce is the term used in the Italian method for crescendoing (growing louder), and decrescendoing (getting softer), on a sustained note. It adjusts the positioning for the proper placement of a note and is particularly effective in the passaggio.

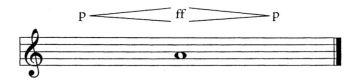

1. Messa di voce can be done on any note and any vowel.
2. Apply positioning for specific registration on each selected note: horizontal for the lower, puckered for the middle, and horizontal for the extreme high.

Use the *noo* vowel for placement in messa di voce to achieve the upper and lower parts of the sound. After placing *oo* with messa di voce, use other vowels in that positioning.

3. Start softly and become louder toward the middle then diminish to the end of the note.

The first part to the crescendo is relatively easy; the last part, or decrescendo, however, takes more control to retain support and placement but is extremely important for ultimate control of the voice. In the decrescendo the tendency is to lift the placement and become shallow with the support. Correct this by keeping the breath in the mouth and supporting with the lower abdomen though the mushroom. *Follow the breath out* instead of pushing at the end of the phrase.

9

Placement for the High Register

The high register is the roof of the voice.
It is the climax of the song.

🎵

The high voice begins from D^1 and goes up to $G^{\#1}$; this range can be a note or two below for lower female voices and an octave lower for male voices. This area is difficult because of the change in voice at E^1 called the passaggio. Use the pucker-abdomen technique for this range as the rounding of the lips allows the apparatus to adjust for the change. This is called *covering the voice*.

▋▋▋ EXERCISE FOR THE HIGH REGISTER

Octave and the third

The octave and the third exercise on the vowels *see-ee yay* is suited to extending the voice into the high range and blending the upper head register with the lower chest range.

see.....................yay...

1. Feel a projection of the breath by yelling "Hey!" on the speech level from the abdomen, as if calling for a taxi.
2. Pucker the lips with the *ee* tongue position as in the previous exercise. (Touch the sides of the tongue to the upper teeth while the tip contacts the lower ones.) Feel as if you are in the high note place with the mushroom before attacking the first note.
3. Pull the lower abdomen in, projecting the high note through the pucker while thinking a two-way stretch.
4. When the lower notes are below the staff, stay in the chest. When the lower notes are in the staff (F), use the mixed head voice. Lower voices adjust according to your lower change of voice.

Release the breath pressure slightly when descending into the chest to prevent a crack or flip, going from one register into the other.

To avoid accenting each note, feel the succession of notes as a round circle, crescendoing on the top note. (Think in two beats, accenting the top and last note instead of stressing every note.)

5. Proceed up the scale by half-steps with this exercise until the top note reaches $G^{\#1}$ above the staff.

Summary
1. Do the pucker-abdomen.
2. Throw the breath through the pucker on a two-way stretch.

VISUALIZATION FOR THE HIGH REGISTER

Singers don't have keys to press in order to control the sound. Therefore, images are vital because you can't get inside and manipulate the vocal apparatus manually; some are pretty strange, but they work. One teacher uses the expression "Flush the toilet!", which is quite amusing but effective. Don't be afraid to explore with images; voice has been taught for hundreds of years with this approach. Images produce a total kinesthetic experience that makes the physical apparatus respond. The following three images are important to visualize in the high range:

1. Visualize the sound and aperture as if singing on the speech level. Use this image instead of reaching for the sound as you ascend to the upper note. The rise in pitch is determined by the speed of vibrations in the vocal folds rather than by the larynx going up and down.

2. Imagine the mouth as a big glob of air. This image is as if you don't have a mouth or throat but that the breath goes through you in the shape of a big glob of air. See the imaginary glob of air as an opening above the head and down to the lower abdomen. Of course, the air can't go through the head and abdomen, but the image will help you extend the sound for the upper and lower resonances and support with the abdomen. Most of all, this helps to release through the muscle instead of straining and holding with the mouth. If you do not do this, you will not be able to reach the note or it will sound flat or shrill.

3. Imagine a two-way stretch, thinking up and down at the same time with the breath when approaching and sustaining a high note.

Summary

1. Imagine—octave, glob, two.

The motto "octave, glob, two" represents: Singing an octave lower on the big glob of air with a two-way stretch. Repeat this phrase and visualize it physically, and gradually the three entities will become one.

APPROACHING HIGH NOTES

Approaching high notes, extend the voice into the upper range on the mushroom, which becomes larger as you reach the extremities in the high range while the bottom becomes smaller (see Figure 2–2).

Come from above, as if already in the high note, instead of reaching from below. Imagine a two-way stretch with the breath, on the speech level. This counteracts reaching.

PLACEMENT FOR THE EXTREME HIGH REGISTER

The extreme high register is the thrill in the voice. It's what "brings the house down." There are three positionings for the three different registers in the voice. The lower chest voice and extreme high register have similar horizontal openings, whereas the middle register is puckered. In the mask technique, retain a horizontal opening for a brighter quality; however, there may be discomfort, if not a real problem, when going through the change in voice at E and E^1 if you don't add a slight pucker to the positioning.

When the top note reaches G#1, change to a horizontal positioning that will help you shift gears into the extreme high register. See next exercise.

▮▮▮ OCTAVE AND THE THIRD EXERCISE

see.....................yay..

1. Position the finger *outside* of your mouth near the molars for an imaginary center of sound.
2. Proceed to the upper note as if you were biting down on the center of a big glob of air, *without biting up.*

Use the image of biting down on a piece of watermelon for the open-horizontal position. Let the lower jaw go back in a chewing motion to form the proper alignment for the upper note.

The *ee* and *ay* vowels (closed vowels) are well suited to this high range. If you are singing *ah* in the high register above the staff, change *ah* to *ay*, which will sound like *ah* in the extreme high register. If it sounds too much like *ay*, keep the *ay* position and sing *ah*.

3. Using this positioning for the high register, think "octave, glob, two," meaning: an octave lower, big glob of air, and a two-way stretch of the breath.
4. Proceed from the lower note into the high with a smooth two-way (up and down) expanding sensation with the breath.

Prepare the approach to the top note with the mushroom in the lower note.

Staying at the center of placement on the molars, glide on a smooth two-way stretch from the lower note into the upper without forcing. At B2 and above, sopranos and tenors direct the breath out the back of the head while expanding down at the same time.

Proceed up the scale in half steps with this exercise until you feel you have reached the limit. Do not strain to expand the range; it will automatically extend as the voice becomes accustomed to the technique.

▪▪▪ LOWER OCTAVE AND THE THIRD

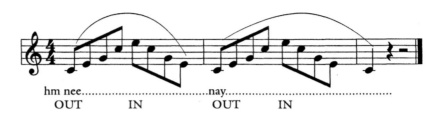

hm nee..nay..
OUT   IN   OUT   IN

Follow the same instructions as in the previous exercise.
1. Use the pucker-abdomen position until the upper note reaches G^1
2. At $A\flat^1$ change to the horizontal opening

The Psychological Gesture for High Notes
The main difference between straight acting and acting in singing is that singers have to sustain musical phrases and long, high notes. The psychological gesture, or PG, is particularly suited for this because it physicalizes intentions for long notes with varied actions. This vocal-dramatic approach is discussed in Part Three.

10

Suggestions for High Notes

Don't reach for high notes
♪

The voice is not spatial—it doesn't have keys to go up and down as do instruments. The vibrations of the vocal folds go faster to raise the pitch and slower to lower the pitch. Therefore, don't reach for high notes, otherwise the vocal apparatus becomes tense and shuts off. Think of singing in the same place that you speak—on the speech level. This is actually where singing takes place—your vocal folds haven't gone up to the top of your head when you hit high C^2 so stay at the speech level.

The following suggestions can ease and free high notes.

APPROACHING HIGH NOTES

Prepare for the high note by coming from above instead of reaching from below. In approaching high notes, the mushroom becomes larger while the bottom becomes smaller. Imagine the breath expanding down and up at the same time in a two-way stretch with the breath, on the speech level, to counteract reaching.

THE BIG-GLOB-OF-AIR IMAGE

Release through the positioning rather than holding with it by imagining the mouth as a big glob of air above the head and down to the chest, thus relieving tension and strain. Crescendo on a high note, hearing with the inner ear and extending the breath into the mushroom on the big glob of air especially in the passaggio (upper change in the voice). Pulling down with the lower muscles can shut off the note when crescendoing.

CLIMAXES

Working up to the climax can produce excessive tension. Make up, or have your teacher make up, special vocalises that cover the same notes of the climaxes in your songs. Include this special vocalise in your daily warm-up so that when you actually sing the climax in the song, you know exactly what to do.

Most singers get nervous at the climax simply because it's the height of the song. Therefore, vocalize climaxes to prepare for singing them in songs.

OVEROPENING

Opening the mouth too widely causes constriction, which prevents rising to the higher notes. High notes whether in the chest or head have to be released. Imagine the positioning for the high note on the speech level first, then sing the note there.

Opening too wide while inhaling can constrict the sound. Overopening also prevents crescendoing because the apparatus cannot be stretched further. For a spontaneous release, imagine the feeling of the attack position with the mouth almost closed, while inhaling.

GO TO THE HIGH NOTE

Go to the high note by leaning forward with the breath to open the throat. At first, slide between the lower and higher note on a two-way stretch to get into the upper note; later, minimize the slide so that it doesn't sound like a scoop. This helps you extend the placement from the lower note instead of reaching for the high note.

Preceding the high note with an *h* can release the breath into the high position; once finding the release, eliminate the *h*.

SUSTAINING HIGH NOTES

Practice approaching high notes in a fast tempo first. The speed gives you the freedom to place the note spontaneously. Once you have experienced the sensation of the placement, sustain the note for two beats. Hold the note longer by adding beat by beat until you have the desired length. Hear and feel the count of the beats as you sustain the note in order to guide the sound instead of holding the note as long as the throat stays open. In this way you tell your voice what to do rather than let your voice direct you.

11

Vocal Problems

As you overcome your vocal problems,
you build your technique.

ᴂ

Voice students experience a number of common problems: singing off pitch, constricting their sound, a shaking in the voice, and tightening of the jaw. Each problem is explained separately. Then a method to overcome vocal tension is given called "The Chewing Method."

PITCH

Staying on pitch is the first prerequisite for singing. Even if you have a beautiful voice, there is no correlation between having a beautiful voice and staying on pitch. If you can't carry a tune, it is useless to pursue a career in singing. Nevertheless, it isn't true that a student doesn't have an ear, if she can't stay on pitch. There are many reasons for going off pitch:

1. Being nervous, especially in the extreme parts of the range
2. Not placing or supporting the voice properly
3. Excessive tension in the production
4. Lack of resonance

It is helpful to take a course in ear training called Sight-Singing, where you learn the difference between pitches and how to read music. This develops the ear and gives an assurance in handling pitches. Resonance affects pitch; you can be on pitch but sound flat without overtones. In all cases, voice lessons should correct going off pitch.

NASALITY

The nasal voice is not a pretty sound. The nose, being a limited resonator, restricts quality and limits abdominal support because the throat is not fully open. Most people—not used to a full sound—resort to settling in the nose. Pop singers tend to sing in the nose, so students feel they have to copy them. However, the pop sound has a better quality and control when placed in the mouth. Some opera singers push into the nose excessively for the ring, but they end up sounding strident.

Reduce nasality by pressing the sides of the nose together so that no sound escapes, and you'll attain immediate resonance in the mouth. After holding the nose throughout an exercise, retain vocal placement by holding the nose every other phrase. Stop holding the nose when the voice stays in the mouth. This gives a fuller, richer quality and connects with breath support.

TREMOLO

When the voice shakes irregularly from the main pitch, it is called a *tremolo*, which is due to lack of placement or support. The voice vibrates out-of-phase with itself, as a car shakes when it is out-of-tune. It is an undesirable quality and weakens the production. Place and support the voice, and the tremolo will disappear.

PUSHING

The biggest problems are holding and pushing muscularly in climactic phrases because of the high notes and excitement in the climax of the song. Tremendous muscular tension is created, like driving a car while pressing the brakes and accelerator at the same time. This expends enormous energy and can make you almost inoperable, particularly in long, high notes. Expand the breath on a two-way stretch to sustain or crescendo. *Follow the breath out* instead of pushing. Getting red in the face is a typical sign of pushing.

TIGHTENING THE JAW

Pulling down too far with the jaw tightens the jaw, constricting and shutting off the sound. Use a chewing motion to close the position and loosen the jaw. See the Chewing Method, page 67.

Chapter Eleven

OVERMOUTHING

Overmouthing tightens the jaw and impedes the sound, inhibiting production, particularly in the upper register of the belted chest voice. If there is excessive tension in overpositioning with the mouth, let the jaw hang loose, then center on the breath; hear and feel the vowel—the muscular positioning will follow automatically. Continue to keep a loose facial position, imagining the positioning on the accented syllables. The accents usually fall on the downbeats (the first beat in each measure).

CRACKING AND BUZZING

Not lifting the soft palate on the attack can cause cracking or buzzing. Also, holding the positioning of the apparatus prevents the note from passing freely, which produces buzzing.

Counteract both by using the BBC breathing technique to follow the breath in and out while singing (see page 86).

EMOTIONAL TENSION

Emotional tension comes from overdoing an action while acting. Repeating the same action restricts the whole process; you will lose volume and power. Vary the action instead; choose gentler actions in the beginning and save more aggressive actions for the climax.

12

The Chewing Method

The chewing method not only relieves vocal tension,
it is also a method for voice production
ৡ

Chewing gives you immediate voice placement. When thinking of the breath as food, it helps you keep the breath more in the mouth. The motion of chewing provides elasticity to the vocal apparatus, producing vibration or resonance. This elasticity allows your ear to adjust to the desired quality reflexively, which is more efficient than positioning cerebrally. It gives mobility to the jaw and tongue, relieving tension. It keeps the center of placement throughout the range.

The chewing method was developed by a famous ear, nose, and throat specialist, Dr. Emil Froeschels, while looking for a holistic method for rehabilitating his nodule and polyp patients. In the beginning, Dr. Froeschels tried different vocal methods but found them all to be partial approaches emphasizing a single aspect of a production instead of the vocal apparatus as a whole.

As he observed people chewing and talking at the same time, he recognized that chewing and speaking involved the same process: They were being done simultaneously. It occurred to him that chewing could be a method for voice production. As he researched further, he discovered that chewing may have been the origin of speech.

Chapter Twelve

■ ■ ■ THE CHEWING TECHNIQUE

1. Place the little finger under the third upper molar from the back, as if biting down on the tip of a bread stick.
2. Grind on the molars using the sound of the nonsense syllable *luv*. You will come into immediate vibration, or instant voice. Leave a little space between the upper and lower molars, as if food were there, giving more space for a bigger sound. Chew as if you were doing a sensory exercise in acting.
3. Add the vowel circle in that chewing place, continuing chewing.
4. Adjust the clarity and resonance of the vowels by ear. As you chew the imaginary breadstick to place the vowels, the apparatus reflexively adjusts to the desired sound while hearing and feeling it.
5. Think of chewing and swallowing the food, which directs the breath in and downward immediately connecting with abdominal support.

Apply chewing in all of the exercises. It is easiest in the chest voice vowel circle. It produces a legato flow to the phrase while singing.

Chewing is particularly effective in the extreme high register where the feeling of biting down, for example, on a piece of watermelon, positions the mouth and jaw for placement.

As you proceed higher in the range, maintain the thought of chewing to retain flexibility of the tongue and jaw.

For extreme high notes, imagine chewing a big glob of air to release muscular tension and prevent overopening.

Summary
1. Place the voice by chewing *luv* on the molars.
2. Chew in the same place while singing.

13

The Master Class

A miniature cosmos where you come in contact
with your strengths and fears.

℘

The best place to practice performing and learn the vocal technique by example is in a Master Class. Private lessons offer an intimate one-to-one study, which is important, especially in the beginning. Later, group classes combined with private lessons are vital so that you can work on scenes with other students. You can also see the technique more objectively when your teacher works with others.

The greatest advantage of a Master Class is that it provides an audience on which to try out your technique and new repertoire. Use the pressure of these little performances to face your fears. This challenge is an opportunity to test your technique and to find strength in yourself. Everyone always says, "Well, I sang it so well this morning in the shower!" Getting nervous challenges you to develop the Technique of the Self, which is learning to control yourself in a performing situation. Singing becomes a vehicle for you to grow.

Don't use auditioning to practice performing or by the time you're ready to audition, you will have created such a bad reputation that few will hear you again. Instead, take the opportunity of a master class to perform and grow in front of a practice audience.

PART THREE

Advanced Technique

14

Coloratura

Fast notes give brilliance and agility
to the voice.

Ornamental notes are rapid scales and embellishments, or fast passages, called *coloratura*. Coloratura is very important for all voices, even heavy voices. It brightens and it lightens the voice, making it easier to handle.

All types of music use rapid scales and embellishments. In classical music this is called coloratura singing. Beverly Sills became famous with this type of singing. Rock singing, rhythm and blues, and jazz use many embellishments on the melodic line called riffing or scatting. Whitney Houston's style is typical of this embellishment.

Hear the passages first by ear. Most people sing fast passages before they know the notes, adjusting with the throat; this causes awkward vocalization by the time you learn the song. Some precede each note with an *h,* giving a harsh quality to fast passages and breaking the melodic line. Rapid figures should be done with a legato—smooth—line and a rhythmic pulse—a light accent on groupings of notes.

The following exercise explains how to hear the notes ahead of time and set the positioning for rapid scales and embellishments according to registration.

∎∎∎ TECHNIQUE FOR LEARNING COLORATURA

First, play

1. Play florid passages slowly and in rhythm on the piano.
   If you do not play the piano, have an accompanist put the florid passages on tape—first slowly, then at the regular speed.
2. Check each interval or group of intervals by looking at the music and hearing the patterns clearly. Listen for where the whole and half steps are.

Next, use a metronome

1. Hear the vowel and notes mentally at a slow tempo, using a metronome, checking notes you are unsure of.
2. Increase the speed gradually until you hear the patterns mentally two notches faster than you are going to sing them.
3. Hear accents on each grouping of notes. For example

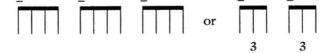

Finally, sing

1. Hearing the notes slightly ahead of a metronome, sing the rapid notes softly and slowly an octave lower. Gradually increase the speed by one notch until you reach the desired tempo.
2. Do not insert *h*'s between notes.

∎∎∎ PLACEMENT

1. Spread the lips, using a horizontal position, feeling the mushroom and the bottom of the sound. Do not use too much bottom, or the sound will be dark and heavy.
2. Sing all passages on *ee.*
3. If the passage is on another vowel, precede *ee* before the other vowel on each accented grouping.
4. Finally, sing the written vowel, hearing and feeling the *ee* position.

This takes a great deal of patience but will produce brilliant coloratura. Few singers can do rapid passages excellently; when done correctly there is a clarity and ring with a height and depth of the sound that is ideal. In opera, Cecilia Bartoli is a master at this. She not only sings coloratura brilliantly but uses it expressively.

A lot of singers sing coloratura without the chest part of the head voice; the sound is with facility but not brilliance. Nevertheless, the head voice is the chief mechanism used for embellished singing. When the voice is too heavy or dark, it is hard to move around.

Summary
1. Place voice in the mask.
2. Sing coloratura with the ear (hearing the notes ahead as you sing them).

COLORATURA VOCALISES

Use the technique for learning coloratura in all the exercises that follow.

■ ■ ■ FAST RUNS

Octave and the fourth

The octave and the fourth scale extends the voice into the extreme high range.

hm nee...................ay...................
OUT...................IN...................

Throw your voice on *oo* from the lower speech level into the falsetto range from the abdomen to sense a projection of the breath.

Progress up the scale by half steps in each try. When the top note reaches $A\flat^1$, change *ah* to *ay*.

▮▮▮ RAPID PASSAGES

Sixteenth note figures

Sixteenth note runs are excellent for agility.

▮▮▮ TRILLS

Whole note trill

The trill is a long note fluctuating rapidly between two notes, it is produced by a loose and swift oscillation of the larynx.

The trill is heard mostly in classical coloratura sopranos.

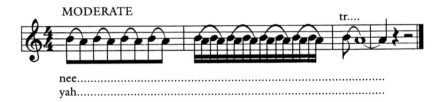

1. Place upper note.
2. Hear the change from pitch to pitch.
3. Start slowly and gradually increase the speed.

The whole note trill provides a clearer distinction between pitches than the half note trill. It gives a higher placement, thus allowing the note to vacillate back and forth more freely.

∎∎∎ TURNS AND GRACE NOTES

A *turn* is an embellished fluctuation starting on the principal note, proceeding above, then to the original note and below, and then returning to the original.

A *grace note* starts on the original note and proceeds either below or above it and returns to the first note.

Turns and grace notes are used in classical as well as pop music.

Summary for coloratura singing

1. Place the note with the mushroom.
2. Make the pitch changes with the ear.

15

Falsetto

Falsetto is the head voice without the chest sound
℘

Falsetto is listed under high notes because it occurs mostly in the extreme high register in male voices. The *falsetto voice* is a straight sound (no vibrato) with a very breathy quality that is best demonstrated by a boy soprano. This lack of vibrato and breathy quality makes it different from the regular head voice without the chest sound, especially in female voices. The vocal folds are highly tensed, extremely stretched, and there is an increased breath flow similar to whistling with the lips.

Theater and pop singing use falsetto more often than classical music. Many shows will call for a rock sound with a falsetto quality in the middle range, using a fuller sound only in climaxes, like "Bring Him Home" from *Les Miserables*. Pop music uses falsetto predominantly with male voices. Females use a light chest voice that sounds like falsetto.

■■■ FALSETTO EXERCISE FOR MALES

For males, after warming up, start at the extreme height of your range, using the fifth leap from D to A; see Falsetto Exercise. Lower voices start a whole step lower.

1. Imitate the quality of a boy soprano with a very straight breathy sound.

2. Slide from the lower note into the upper on *ee* or on whichever vowel is easier for you.

3. Proceed up the scale by half steps as far as you feel comfortable.

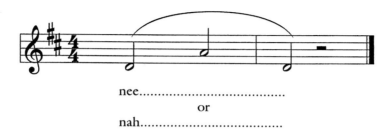

nee..
or
nah..

Keep the mouth relaxed and don't strain; let the voice rise easily as if on the speech level.

For a fuller falsetto sound, bring the breath down into the mouth; it will begin to sound like a rich female alto voice. This is the sound used by the operatic female impersonator in *Chicago*.

Falsetto in females is an undesirable quality. Very light sopranos sing naturally in falsetto until they are trained to add chest voice. The falsetto quality is lifted in placement without vibrato and is often called a white sound. When chest is added, it becomes the head voice that is the desired quality for the legitimate soprano voice. It brings in a richness of vibrato that produces a strong and beautiful resonant sound.

Falsetto in females is used only for character voices in musical theater. Rock and folk singing use a very light chest voice that sounds like falsetto.

16

Adapting the Opera Voice to Musical Theater

A vocal method is necessary to meld the two mediums
of opera and musical theater

℘

This book uses classical technique as a basis for musical theater sound. Adapting the opera voice to musical theater can be done quite easily—you need only to modify the quality of the sound. The major adjustment is a technique for the pure chest voice—where the chest voice alone is used without a mixture of head and chest. The classical approach for the pure chest voice in this book protects the voice from the strain that is so feared by opera singers. Style, diction, and acting need to be adjusted as well. Techniques for these changes are covered below.

VOCAL TECHNIQUE

In changing the opera voice to suit musical theater, adapt the vocal technique by using a more frontal production in the mask. Next, minimize the vibrato.

Every medium has its own sound, but in musical theater you run the gamut of vocal quality from Broadway, pop, rock, and jazz to opera. The technique has to be adjusted to suit each medium as you adapt your quality to each style. In singing for musical theater, pop, rock, and jazz, the foundation is based on the pure chest voice.

Pure Chest Voice

Many famous opera singers do musical theater recordings; however, they do not change the quality of their voices to suit the style. They lighten their voices but still do not adapt the quality of the sound. They sing in a high range not suited to Broadway and avoid the use of pure chest voice in the middle range that is indicative of musical theater. Donal Henahan's article "More on 'Belting' in the Opera House" in the *New York Times* quotes from a letter I sent him in response to his preceding article "Why Can't Verdi Voices Handle Sondheim?"

> The reason why opera voices can't handle Sondheim is in register and tessitura. Most music for musical theater is written in the weakest part of the singer's range, e.g., the soprano's change of voice between middle C and C^1 [the C above middle C]. The chest voice and legit head voice have to be melded into one sound. Most Broadway singers are not trained to do this, so they resort to carrying the chest voice up through the head range. This belted sound is strong and exciting in an otherwise weak middle range. The mixed legit sound cannot compare with the aggressiveness and clarity of the belted sound in this range.

MELDING OPERA AND MUSICAL THEATER

Classical singers and musical theater vocalists have long been at odds with each other. Their vocal approaches are at opposite poles. Opera singers tend to be overly vocal, while musical theater actors abuse the voice by yelling until they create nodes on their vocal folds. There is a snobbishness on both sides, yet each could learn from the other.

I remember how I frowned on musical theater when I was studying at Juilliard. Later, having been a classical recitalist for many years, when I got the part of Helen Chiao in *The Flower Drum Song* by Rodgers and Hammerstein, I felt that musical theater was beneath me. During the tryout in Boston, night after night I kept getting the note, "Too operatic!" One day after rehearsal, I asked Richard Rodgers if he would coach me note for note on the song "Love, Look Away," which was written for me. I told him that all my training was in opera, so I didn't know any other approach. He was a man of few words and said, "O.K."

Several days later he brought in a coach from New York. We worked all afternoon. That evening, after the show, Hammerstein came up to my dressing room and said, "That was wonderful! Do you know what you're doing?" I answered, "Yes." It was a matter of not using too much vibrato and allowing the acting to be the guide instead of letting the voice dominate the production. I had simplified the body movement, keeping big gestures for the climax of the song. I also concentrated on my "inner life" (the inner life is the action from the scene that takes place in your mind) and directed it out to my imaginary partner. So, as an operatically trained singer, I had to learn to adjust to the style of singing for musical theater. My snobbishness was uncalled for.

From this experience I have learned that a vocal method is necessary to meld the two mediums of opera and musical theater, combining the beauty of vocalism in opera and the dramatic communication in musical theater.

Pop Style

Classical singers also make records of pop songs; here again, they do not use the proper sound for the style. The quality of pop singing is breathy and is sung in the lower register. Both of these aspects are opposite to those used in opera singing. The breathy sound and lower keys used in pop singing produce a natural spoken sound and give an intimacy that the legitimate sound doesn't have. This was brought about by the use of the microphone upon which opera singers frown. The spoken character of the amplified voice, however, is the main essence of pop music. Thus, when opera singers retain the legitimate sound and sing in high keys, it is like a fish out of water. It would be as if Frank Sinatra sang the aria, "Ridi, Pagliacci!"

When I had my cabaret act, I discovered the values in jazz singing—the talent of a natural ear and feeling for rhythm. Being able to change the written rhythms in jazz to my individual interpretation was a completely different experience from a rigid rhythmic training classically.

Diction

It has always been hard to understand opera singers when they are singing. Italian is more favorable to them because the vowels are pure, whereas English has subtleties of speech melody that include the use of the stressed and unstressed syllable (pronounced *uh*). For example, in the song "I'm Going to Sit Right Down and Write Myself a Letter," the pop enunciation would be, "Uhm gonnuh sit right down uhnd write muhself uh lettuh." A classical singer would find that speech far beneath him. They pronounce every syllable as written, with the same stress; their diction still sounds operatic (often with a foreign accent as well) and is marred not only by the accent but also by an overvocal production. Too much vibrato not only is out of place, but it also obscures the enunciation. Yet, if you're going to sing pop music, the proper diction and sound create the style.

Another point in pop music is that written rhythms have to be changed to approximate speaking rhythms because the singer follows speech rhythms with the use of stressed and unstressed syllables. If you don't do this, you are considered square.

Because musical theater, too, is based on the spoken sound, the words are as important as the music—at times, more important. It is desirable in musical theater to go directly from the spoken dialogue into the song without a change in vocal quality. John Raitt, in *Carousel*, shows a wonderful example of this in his rendition of "If I Loved You." You aren't even aware that he has begun singing (see Diction, page 50).

Acting

The New York State Theater is training their opera singers to be skilled actors. Still, on the whole (unless you are a Maria Callas or Teresa Stratas), acting in opera remains a matter of indicated actions and stiff body movement. In musical theater, there is a reality of communication that comes from the trained actor that is indispensable. Not only is the acting important, sometimes it is more crucial than the music. In musical theater, an actor who can sing fairly well will get the job over a beautiful singer who can't act. Steven Sonheim, the famous musical theater composer, prefers the actor-singer to the singer-singer.

A formal acting technique enhances your interpretation and actually helps you to physically produce sound. It gives you the intention of the scene, sends you into action mentally and physically, guides your eye focus, and produces body movement. In the end it gives you depth, identity, confidence, and conviction. It makes you an artist.

The Opera Singer's Contribution

It is important that opera singers do musical theater. The time is ripe for the two fields to meld. The classical singer brings a vocal richness seldom achieved in musical theater. The intention of this book is to present a method that is based on a classical technique that has been modified for musical theater, melding the best of both media.

The opera voice *can* learn to sound in the specific style of music from Broadway to pop, rock, and jazz. The opera singer needs to be open to varying vocal quality and to accepting that size and resonance are not always the main goal in singing.

The main difference in singing styles is determined by varying degrees of the use of pure chest voice and increasing or decreasing resonance. There is a vocal spectrum with the opera singer at one end and the soft rock singer at the other: opera—light opera—legitimate musical theater (Rodgers and Hammerstein)—jazz—pop—rock. The opera sound is the fullest and most resonant in size and quality; at the other end of the spectrum, the soft rock singer uses the pure chest voice with a light, breathy sound. Thus, by lessening resonance through a more frontal-mask placement, controlling vibrato, and a fuller use of pure chest voice, the opera singer can produce the sound for each medium.

17

Advanced Stages of Singing

The semiconcious level—
learning to juggle multiple techniques
℘

In the beginning, it is necessary to form vowels physically to achieve quality, volume, and range. In the Advanced Stages of Singing, allow the whole process to be reflexive, as singing is the most efficient at a kinesthetic and auditory level. As in dancing or playing golf, the brain is too slow to bring together the multiple adjustments to operate the mechanism efficiently.

An exercise called the BBC (Blank, Breath, Center) allows placement and breathing from the abdomen to come together reflexively. It is the most important technique in controlling the breath. To inhale, relax and let the breath breathe you as you follow the breath in, then follow the breath out as you sing. This allows a kinesthetic experience to take place, supporting the sound more efficiently in contrast to managing the breath muscularly. Using the BBC also prepares you for the attack and provides placement and support by being centered on the breath. The mushroom and the bottom of the sound come together automatically by feeling the shape of the sound centered on the breath. There is more control and resonance as you follow the breath out versus pushing it out abdominally. Less tension in the jaw, mouth, and tongue results because the apparatus functions as a complete unit instead of as separate parts.

The BBC aids the beginner as well as the advanced singer. Think of it before the attack of the sound, rather than the actual sound itself. As you become more skilled you will be able to do the BBC more quickly, and it can be realized in just the intake of the breath at a semiconcious level.

▪▪▪ BREATHING AND MEDITATIVE EXERCISE

The BBC

Use the BBC, a simple meditative process, to relax excessive tension, direct your breathing, and center your concentration.
1. Make your mind a blank. The first *B* represents the word *blank,* releasing muscular tensions in your body.
2. The second *B* means *breath.* Let go of muscular tensions, and the breath will come to you, as opposed to consciously stretching the chest and abdominal muscles to breathe.
3. *C* means *center.* Follow and center your voice on that breath.

Summary
BBC means Blank, Breath, Center.

THE NEED FOR ACTING IN SINGING

The next step in Advanced Singing is *finding the scene in the song,* or acting in singing. Acting intentions spontaneously produce phrasing (the manner in which you sing the melody), dynamics, physical movement, and eye focus. The scene in the song is created from a special need within yourself; therefore, the song is your own. A coach can tell you how to phrase and move physically, even demonstrate for you, but discovering this yourself makes you an individual artist.

The subject of acting in singing could cover several volumes. The following, however, are some simple tools to explain how acting aids in producing vocal sound:

▪▪▪ ACTING EXERCISE

To find the scene in the song, use the following three steps:
1. An objective—What do you want to achieve in the scene?
   (What are you fighting for?)

2. An obstacle—Who or what is preventing you from achieving the objective?
3. A physical task—What are you doing physically while trying to achieve your objective? Are you sweeping the floor or are you drinking coffee?

An action is what you do physically to achieve your objective; actions affect the use of your voice and body. Your objective, obstacle, and task send you into action in your scene. When you say the phrase "Come here," the physical action may be to draw the person to you that comes automatically from your acting intention. The action produces the sound physically by bringing in the use of your body to draw the object to you with your voice.

An infinite variety of dynamics occur through playing actions. In a soft passage, if you're whispering in your lover's ear, you'll naturally use a soft sound. Concentrating on singing softly or loudly takes you out of the scene because you're observing how loudly or softly you're singing instead of concentrating on your intention.

Another advantage from the scene is spontaneity, permitting you to be creative rather than "canned." Spontaneity is important for freedom and fulfillment of expression because each moment in the scene should be a new discovery. When you predetermine how a line or lyric should be read or sung, you "can" your performance, presetting your delivery, which only makes you self-conscious because you wonder if you are duplicating that reading.

Thus, acting is a vital technique in singing. It gives you the message of what you're singing about, thereby producing your intentions and actions. These actions direct the use of your body, creating a physical life for the scene, and they physically produce the sound. This psychophysicalization of action in sound is "Advanced *Vocal* Technique".

▪▪▪ COMBINING VOICE WITH ACTING (VAP)

Combining acting with singing is a complicated process. When students first start to put acting and singing together, the tendency is to lose both skills. It is similar to juggling: when you add a second pin, you will probably drop both. Practice, patience, and time bring the two disciplines together. In order to achieve this multiple procedure, use the symbol VAP (Vowel, Action, Partner) to bring the voice and acting together:

1. *V* represents the vowel that brings together your voice placement and support.
2. *A* is the action directed to your partner. Use a physically active verb like *kiss, push,* or *caress.*
3. *P* is the partner.

Music is mood producing, causing you to direct feelings inward, creating an emotional orgy with yourself. Having a scene projects your acting intentions outward to your partner, which the audience sees as acting. It also determines your speech, dynamics, phrasing, and operation of breath.

Summary
VAP represents Vowel, Action, Partner.

THE PSYCHOLOGICAL GESTURE FOR HIGH NOTES

The main difference between straight acting and acting in singing is that singers have to carry a musical line or melody. This is even more complicated when you have to sustain long, high notes. The psychological gesture is particularly suited for this.

The Psychological Gesture was created by Michael Chekhov, who claims that the kind of movement you make gives your willpower a certain direction. The physical gesture will awaken and animate in you a definite desire, want, or wish.

Advanced vocal technique comes from a combination of vocal production and a need to express yourself. Play an action such as shoving, and the physical adjustment to produce the note will be created. For example, throwing your partner out might be played in a loud voice caused by a physical shove from you. This psychophysiological process produces the sound and is Advanced Vocal Technique. Making a loud sound without the emotional need will not be nearly as efficient or expressive as the psychophysiological production from acting. The voice becomes a vehicle to express yourself and not an end in itself.

Long, held notes are physicalized through the Psychological Gesture with varied actions.

Technique for the Psychological Gesture

When the sustained note is a very long one, anywhere from four to eight measures—sometimes even more—use two to three different actions consecutively. If you're sustaining the note on the word *love,* you may

- reach out
- pull the person to you
- embrace at the end of the note

▮▮▮ EXERCISE FOR THE PSYCHOLOGICAL GESTURE

1. Act out the different actions physically, as you verbalize the varied subtexts. For the word *love* you may have three different subtexts as follows:
   a. "You mean so much to me."—Use the action to reach out.
   b. "Let me hold you."—Pull the person to you.
   c. "I've waited all my life for you."—Embrace the person.
2. Vocalize those three actions consecutively on the vowel of the word in the lyrics. In this case, the vowel in *love* is an *uh* sound; for a better quality say *uh* in the *ah* place. Physicalize the actions to reach, pull toward you, and embrace as you vocalize *ah* on the speech level. To sustain the gesture, feel as if you're pushing through sand.
3. Vocalize *love* on the speech level while physicalizing the progressive actions.
4. Sing *love* on the actual note in the song while physicalizing the progressive actions.

This psychological gesture will physically sustain the note and tell you how to use your body while holding the note. Most singers stand there, with hands at their sides, becoming tense, wanting to use their body but not knowing how. Thus, the psychological gesture produces, physicalizes, expresses, and frees the high note. This vocal and dramatic approach produces a need for high notes; in fact, when the desire is great, the note is not even high enough. So, instead of fearing the high note, you will welcome the opportunity to rise to the heights to express yourself.

18

Zen in the Art of Studying Singing

A man who has attained mastery of an art
reveals it in his every action.
—Samurai maxim
ℰℐ

Let the vehicle of singing help you break through the shell of your fear and find a way of life. "Zen in the Art of Studying Singing" is the technique of life.

THE NOVICE

When first studying voice as a student, there is a childlike joy of discovering a new experience. Few demands are required while uncovering unknown skills. Singing along to the radio with ease and confidence, your future seems bright.

The more advanced you become, the more skills you acquire. Now you are responsible to use those skills: The playing has gone, and you have to deliver! You wonder, "What has happened to the song I picked up for the first time and sang like a dream?" Self-doubt begins.

Singing well once is a credit to your talent, but performing well time after time is a credit to your technique. Skills do not come easily: In order to develop through study, hard work, and patience, you have to learn how to learn.

Singers frequently are impatient, lack discipline, and expect miracles after a few lessons. Many ask for few lessons to prepare for an audition or a singing part in a show: They are looking for a quick fix.

THE SERIOUS STUDENT

The serious student needs to develop the right attitude in learning how to study. The following is a method of learning how to learn:

SIX ASPECTS OF PERSONAL DEVELOPMENT
1. Personality problems
2. The Eastern student
3. Meditation to improve learning skills
4. Energized concentration
5. Technique of the self
6. Technique of life

PERSONALITY PROBLEMS

The first step is to be open-minded and honest so you can become aware of problems that affect you. Most students are plagued by impatience, their egos, and their frustrations in aiming for perfection.

Impatience

Impatience is common among students and is the most difficult of the three to overcome: Many beginning students don't understand why it takes so much time and effort to learn to sing a simple song. Unprepared and impatient to perform, they don't realize that they are not ready and that lasting skills take time to learn and to develop.

Seasoned performers study and continue coaching lessons throughout their careers to keep their skills in top shape. This helps them maintain the high standards needed for nightly performances that extend into months— sometime even years—during demanding worldwide schedules. They must also perform when they are ill or are in a bad mood.

If you are to meet these situations, train to master the skills that make that possible. Inevitably, when I have gotten a student to conquer a certain aspect of the technique he or she couldn't do moments before, the student will say, "I hope I can do that again." That is a negative approach that causes impatience.

Develop a positive attitude toward your growth process; build on your experience instead of negating it. Instead of being impatient, appreciate what you've learned and say, "Wow, that's what does it! Let's do it again!" This approach will produce confidence; the negative approach is destructive. Acquiring the proper attitude and technique is more important than learning to sing a song.

One of the reasons we tend to be impatient is that we think we know more than we really do. We can have grandiose ideas about ourselves and our talent without even being aware of it. Understanding yourself is as important as knowing how to sing. No matter how much you know, if you are unable to put that knowledge into practice, then the knowledge is useless. Realize that

Information is only knowledge.

Putting that knowledge into practice is enlightenment.

The true goal in all of the arts is to know yourself.

Know yourself by understanding your personal character—inclinations, habits, weaknesses, and strengths—so that you can overcome difficult personality problems that slow your growth.

Realize that there is a difference between who you really are and the fantasy of who you think you are. There is a difference between a dream and a fantasy; in striving for your dream, you must dive in and do the work to earn that dream. You need to do your job to hone skills with patience. In fantasy, you live in your imagination, never achieving anything but a state of ignorance. It is said, "Ignorance is bliss." This is living in a fantasy that is self-defeating. It's like the housewife who sits home and fantasizes about being a movie star without having any idea of the work involved. Therefore, understand yourself so that you can be patient.

If you feel impatient and frustrated because you cannot master a certain technique, then have it out with yourself; get it out of your system: Even if you have to curse, feel disgusted, and even have a private temper tantrum. Give up for a day. Then let it go, and get back to doing your job. Better still laugh at yourself and say, "O.K., stop goofing off and get on with doing your job" or "I see technically what to do now." When you learn not only to do your job but to love the work, then you will become a singer.

The Ego

The ego is how we perceive ourselves. It determines how we fit into the world around us and how circumstances affect our behavior. To be objective as a performer is hard because our performance is being constantly judged; that makes us vulnerable. Self-conscious about how well or poorly we do, we end up feeling either overly egotistical or painfully inferior. Afraid of failure, or even of success, we refuse to tackle the job at hand, thinking that by not acting we have not failed.

Fear of failure is defeating because competition is necessary in the life of a singer. The need to be the best does not help a performer. At an audition, when you sing well, you're puffed up and preening about getting a call back. Or if the reverse happens, you don't do well and want to shrink and disappear. Not being the best or among the best, destroys your incentive to go on. However, you can't always be the best, there is inevitably someone better; therefore, you end up feeling frustrated.

To control this vicious circle you have to realize how the ego works. The ego is controlled by our conception of life: Why are you here? How do you fit in the world and with those around you?

Understanding yourself in terms of your needs will help you find your true self. Be humble and discover who you really are. This requires patience. Instead of moaning over how well you sang at home—even though you couldn't do as well in class—learn from your mistakes. Rejoice that you're not ignorant anymore. Ignorance is not bliss—waking up to reality is! Jesus said, "Ye shall know the Truth and the Truth shall make you free!" Your truth lies in the discovery of your self and in overcoming your faults. When you can achieve something you never did before, you will be freed from the bonds of your ignorance.

Aiming for Perfection

Striving for perfection can only frustrate you because trying to be perfect is results oriented. Being results oriented is setting your mind on the outcome of what you're doing instead of concentrating on how to achieve it. Concentrate on the technique to make it perfect, and then you can achieve the means that produces perfection. It is said:

> When one eye is fixed upon your destination there is only one eye left with which to find the way.
>
> —Anonymous

This means you must concentrate on your vocal technique to do the job (the way) that will get you to perfection (your destination). If you think only of achieving perfection, there is no method with which to get you there. So, go for the process, not the result.

Summary

Impatience, ego, and perfection get in the way of learning; they slow down the process.

Impatience wastes energy because negativity obscures your constructive attitude toward learning.

The real ego has to be recognized in order to adjust to your specific stage of growth.

Also, perfection has to give way to the process of attaining it by applying your vocal technique.

THE EASTERN STUDENT

The Eastern religions and philosophies develop strength of character by teaching singing, dancing, or tennis as the only vehicles to experience and growth. Taking on a new experience challenges our confidence. For a serious student, the steps in building that confidence are more important than getting a job from an audition or winning a tennis match. The aim is to develop your character in order to apply your knowledge. Strengthening yourself through the vehicle of singing becomes foremost.

Therefore, it's not the singing of a song, it is conquering your fears, doubts, and dreams that is the goal.

MEDITATION TO IMPROVE LEARNING SKILLS

In the martial arts, because skills are useless unless you have the discipline to apply them, the master prepares the mind as well as the physical technique of fighting

To control the mind, first, humble yourself by emptying your mind in order to make room for new information. At a voice lesson, don't be so wrapped up in your ideas that only half of the suggestions your teacher makes are heard. The saying goes, "If your cup is too full, there is no room for more."

Next, have the right goal as a student. The Western approach tends to be results oriented, which means getting the job, being famous, or being rich.

Eastern philosophies and religions, on the other hand, teach letting go of worldly values and finding a peace and center within yourself. That peace enables you to see objectively and to concentrate on the job at hand. Having a center within yourself is knowing who you are and what you want in life. This strengthens you.

The right attitude in a student is essential before a Zen Master will accept the student. The following is a story of a student seeking a Master to learn swordsmanship.

A ZEN STORY OF SWORDSMANSHIP

A student, anxious to become a swordsman, asks a Master how long will it take to study swordsmanship if he works very hard. The Master answers, "Ten years."

The student thinks that's much too long, so he asks, "If I study day and night how long will it take?"

The Master smiles and says, "Twenty years."

The student, flabbergasted, draws a deep breath, inquiring, "If I study day and night and sleep on it, how long will it take?"

The Master frowns and says, "Thirty years!"

This is a puzzlement for the student, who thinks that the harder he works, the more successful he will be. He doesn't realize that a student's proper attitude is as important as the effort. But, because he is desperate to study with the Master, he finally agrees to do anything the Master says.

The next day, ready and willing, the student anxiously waits for his first assignment. The Master gives him a pail and brush to scrub the floor. The student wonders what this has to do with swordsmanship, but accepts the scrubbing, hating every moment of it. Day after day he scrubs; the Master ignores him. He resents scrubbing and gives vent to his anger and scrubs harder. The floor becomes very clean. The student suddenly notices that the floor starts to shine and says, "Hey, this looks good." He begins to enjoy scrubbing.

One day, humming and scrubbing happily, he suddenly feels a hit on the head from nowhere. These sudden and unexpected attacks continue for days on end.

Finally, he is able to sense and avoid the attacks coming from the master. The master then presents the sword to him and says, "Now, you are ready to study swordsmanship."

ZEN STORY LESSON

1. Scrubbing the floor—Acquire a humbled devotion for work; even develop a great love for it. In singing, instead of demanding that you become a proficient singer in one or two years, humble yourself and accept whatever time it takes.
2. Being hit on the head out of nowhere—Be open and alert so that you can take from your environment. Empty your cup and let the teacher fill your mind.
3. A student must be humble and patient before a Zen Master will consider him as a student. After you have acquired the right attitude in becoming a serious student, the next step is to control your mind, which is found in meditation.

Meditation

Meditation, in its simplest form, is for quieting yourself and relaxing the body to control your mind more effectively. Meditation is turning off your thoughts or making your mind a blank; in this state the mind rests, and you feel a state of peace.

▪▪▪ MEDITATION EXERCISE

1. Sit with your backbone straight and with your head aligned over your spine comfortably. Sit in a straight-backed chair with your feet on the floor or in the lotus position with your legs crossed over each other. Rest your hands comfortably on your thighs with the palms down.
2. Consciously release rigid muscles one by one in your brow, neck, back, and so on. You can even relax your brain by thinking of letting go of the tension in it.
3. As you relax your muscles, your breath will come to you. Follow that inhalation instead of making yourself breathe.
4. Repeat the word "Om" slowly in your mind.
5. Don't let random thoughts bother you. Just repeat the word "Om," which in Eastern religion is the primal sound from which the entire universe emanates and is the inner essence of

all mantras. It guides, empowers, and heals. Repeat it in your mind, and it will strengthen you and will stop distracting thoughts (thoughts of what you have to do next, conflicts that disturb you, and so forth). If you hear outer noises, street noises, neighbors, don't let them bother you; let them go through you. Don't fight noises, random thoughts, or your inability to turn them off. Just say, "O.K.," and go back to the word "Om".

6. After twenty minutes of meditating, take one minute to open your eyes to come out. Meditate twice a day for twenty minutes before breakfast and before dinner. If you meditate after you eat, you will tend to go to sleep.

In some way, we all do a kind of meditation in our everyday lives. Whenever we concentrate on a particular subject, we are meditating. Thoughts are determined by your devotion in life. Therefore, it is important to know what you want in life because that determines what you think and who you are.

Most people find it difficult to relax and quiet themselves during meditation. They say, "I can't meditate! My mind is everywhere. How can I not think of anything?" The Chinese have a saying, "The mind jumps around like a monkey in a tree."

It is true that the mind is filled with thoughts. Nevertheless, you can learn to control your mind; do this through devotion. If your dreams in life are strong enough, you will be riveted to those desires. Truly wanting peace and a connection with a Power within yourself will enable you to meditate on only that.

The act of meditating is just doing it and not being disturbed by random thoughts. Any attempt you make is successful. In the least, meditation can give you a sense of rest/peace; at its fullest it can connect with a powerful energy within yourself. Channel this strength into your work through an energized concentration.

ENERGIZED CONCENTRATION

Energized concentration is a super power or inner strength available to everyone. In everyday life, it is usually experienced in cases of emergency. When a mother is able to break down a heavy door to get to her child in a burning room, this is an act of that super power.

When your intentions are riveted on your goal, that is energized concentration. In order to achieve this in your singing, combine the ideals in your life—personal goals, dreams, overcoming shortcomings—with the acting objective in your scene.

For example, in the song "Tonight" from *Westside Story* Maria is preparing herself to see Tony. You may use the substitution of preparing for an audition. (A substitution is an actual experience from your own life that has the same intentions of the character in the scene.) Your substitution must be of the utmost urgency—what you would live or die for—to draw upon this inner strength.

In the Sunday *New York Times*, November 18, 1994, David Richards said about Glenn Close in *Sunset Boulevard*, "The actress takes breath-taking risks, venturing so far out on a limb at times that you fear it will snap. It doesn't."

Her need to find the key to playing the character is more urgent than the need to be right. She's willing to go for broke.

This difference of going all the way is what separates a great performer from a good one. Good performers are always standing outside of themselves, checking to see if they are good. Great artists will go all the way, not caring how it looks or feels. They run the risk of being way off, but ninety percent of the time they are right on and reach the heights. Good performers never go beyond being good because they are always observing themselves. This limits the good performer; you cannot be outside observing and inside doing at the same time.

This total commitment of a great artist produces energized concentration. In an emergency or moments of great need, the mind and body coordinate with tremendous strength that results in inspiration.

TECHNIQUE OF THE SELF

Psycho-Cybernetics, or Self-image Through Visualization

Psycho-cybernetics, a type of meditation, is a technique for mind control through visualization. Become aware of the aspects of your personality, then use psycho-cybernetics to minimize your failings and to maximize your desired state of being through visualization. Psycho-cybernetics was mentioned in the chapter "How to Practice" and is repeated here. This most effective way of practicing was discovered by Dr. Maxwell Maltz.

Dr. Maltz says, "Experimental and clinical psychologists have proved beyond a shadow of a doubt that the human nervous system cannot tell the difference between an actual experience and an experience imagined vividly and in detail. When you experience, something happens inside your nervous system and your mid-brain. New engrams and neural patterns are recorded in the gray matter of your brain."

Dr. Maltz suggests imagining the complete experience before doing it. So in singing, you will have practiced the steps already; therefore, the correct response will be more immediate.

As preparation for visualization, do the simple meditative BBC exercise, relieving your mental and muscular tensions (see page 86).

The BBC exercise is particularly helpful whenever you are nervous, as before an audition or going onstage. Do the BBC, then visualize the state that you want to be in—relaxed, ready, and assured. Next, imagine yourself in the opposite state—nervous, anxious, listless. Feel how the body responds differently when imagining positive thoughts or negative ones. This is caused not only by your mental state but also by a chemical reaction to your thoughts. When you have positive thoughts, the body produces a healing chemical reaction, and when you have negative thoughts the opposite happens. As we have all experienced, we can actually feel ill by just thinking about something unpleasant.

This is how prayer helps and heals us, as we give ourselves to a higher power to bring about a connection with a Positive Energy.

Many of the greatest personalities possess a strength and conviction through religion that helps them face the toughest problems. Thought in prayer connects them with a special Power and produces an energized concentration producing super strength.

To connect with your inner power, use psycho-cybernetics to do the following:

1. Do the BBC.
2. Visualize your desired self-image.

Learn to think positively with visualization. Relish what you're learning instead of considering it a chore. My father, who's 101 and quite a wise man, says, "Life can take everything away from you but your education. You can lose your family, money, job, lover, but once you are educated that education will always be with you."

When you learn to love the job at hand and not be results oriented, you will have found your center. Your center is knowing who you are and what you are living for—your convictions in life. It is the real you. Believe in what you have discovered and have a need to share that with others, then you will have charisma. The dictionary defines "charisma" as a divinely inspired gift, grace, or talent. This intimates that you have to be born with charisma and that it's not nurtured or developed. We all, however, have a certain gifts or talents. When you have a need to share that talent, you will have charisma.

Once you have developed your self-image, the aim is to find yourself through control, in order to live the fullest life. Since singing is only a vehicle to develop your character, singing becomes a way to find yourself. This maturing through self-control becomes the "Technique of Life" which brings us to the sixth and last step.

TECHNIQUE OF LIFE

The technique of life is learning how to develop character. Whatever goal we strive for—be it love, fame, or fortune—that goal becomes only a vehicle to become aware of our weaknesses and to find our strengths. In this case, the vehicle is the technique of singing. The achievement is in the process or steps, not in the goal itself. It is conquering the steps in our journey, not the arrival, that improves our character.

"Zen in the Art of Studying Singing" deals with the first step in learning: self-doubt. Self-doubt comes from the dualism of the mind. You feel this when you start to perform: You are at the mercy of everybody's criticism, so you have to be on your mettle and deliver. Having to perform at a high level, makes self-doubt loom heavily over you. Often, the first thought that comes to mind before you start to sing is, "I hope I can do this well" or "This is probably not going to turn out the way I want."

To understand self-doubt, we have to ask ourselves, "What is the reason for Life?" To some, it seems the reason for being alive is to overcome the dualism of the mind or to conquer the negative traits within us. That negative part of our mind is the little man who sits on your shoulder saying, "You can't do that! You're not good enough!"

The purpose in living is to tame your negative thoughts or at least put them in their place, where they don't get the better of you. The saying "Get thee behind me devil!" has an immediate effect on your singing because success or failure is determined by the control of your attitude.

The Yin and the Yang

The Chinese believe, however, that the negative mind is a part of life. They call it the Yin and the Yang. The Yin is the passive, negative female force, and the Yang is the active, positive male force. Together they make up the whole of life, working harmoniously with each other. You can balance the negative and positive experiences in your life by getting negative experiences to work for you. You will then be in control.

Understanding Nervousness

One of the greatest fears in singing is losing approval. If we don't sing well, we are afraid that we will lose the respect and love of others. That is why much of the nervousness in singing comes from the fear that is associated with the loss of that love. If we didn't love, we wouldn't fear the loss of that love. In order to conquer this, use whatever you feel—fear, love, impatience, or anxiety—in all of your scenes. Fear becomes your obstacle, preventing you from achieving what you want. For instance, in your scene, if you want to win over your partner, who is your obstacle, your personal substitution for the obstacle can be your own fears. The substitution for your main objective then is to conquer your fears.

This is a prime example of what the Chinese call the Yin and the Yang—good and evil, male and female, and love and hate (the fear from the loss of that love), which are all part of life.

Instead of suppressing your fear, include it in the scene, and you will find a new strength in using your fear. This is similar to acting out scenes in psychotherapy: Get rid of your frustrations by expressing them and in the process develop courage. We all know how powerful fear is. Using it in a scene can free you, whereas suppressing it will only make it loom larger. Good and evil will always be present but realize that you have a choice between the two! Make use of evil, instead of letting it conquer you, then you become one or whole.

The great meditation master, Gurumayi Chidvilasananda from The Syda Foundation said:

> Until what we think, feel, and do are one we have no power or effectiveness in our life.

Steven Sondheim is a wonderful example of overcoming negative experiences. In a recent article, he said his mother, before going into heart surgery, sent him a hand-delivered letter because she thought she was going to die and wanted to make sure that he got it. She said, "You are the worst thing that happened to me in my life!" With such a crushing remark from the one of the most important people in his life, he certainly had to develop a strong character. In fact, he seems to have used that in his musicals; many of them are moralistic. Remember the lines from *Into the Woods,* "No one is alone" and "Careful the things you say, children will listen."

Going for a result like getting the job or being perfect can only make you self-conscious because you are watching to see if you're making an impression or being perfect. Therefore, go for the process—the technique—and the result of getting the job or perfection will follow.

With this goal in mind, you will find your concentration improves and you will start to earn confidence. This growth is the development of your character. Because of this personal and technical accomplishment you will mature in life through the process of learning how to sing.

There is a greater demand personally in being an artist than there is in holding an average job. Therefore, artists tend to have a higher awareness and sensitivity about life than the average person. This higher awareness makes you search for the center of your inner convictions that nurture confidence, commitment, and charisma.

So, with new strength of character, break through the shell of your fear and become whole. Remember, it is more than singing; singing is not only the vehicle to help you be whole, it becomes a way of life!

Remember the Samurai maxim,

> A man who has attained mastery of an art reveals it in his every action.

19

Stages of Growth

Experience produces the professional.

§Ɔ

The stages you go through in your development will bring up many adjustments and challenges. Don't be discouraged. Singing is not only learning a technique it is applying it. This is where experience comes in.

EXPERIENCE

As you go through the learning process, analyze what it is that helps you sing well. This eventually becomes your technique. Many times in studying a particular aspect of the technique and conquering it, you achieve what you want. If you concentrate only on the outcome instead of the production, you will lose that effect. Therefore, be aware of technique, not just the results.

It is this very process that makes the difference between the inexperienced student and professional, who has gone through the fire of sifting out the real solidity of the technique. When you really know what works for you, then you will become professionally competent.

MISTAKES AND RECOVERY

When practicing, it is natural to stop and correct yourself. At the end of your practice period, however, give yourself a run-through of your song. Don't stop, regardless of how many mistakes you make. If you forget the words, just use *la, la,* until you finish the song. Learning to recover from your mistakes is important because in performance you cannot stop and start over again. Everyone makes mistakes; it is learning how to recover that makes you professional.

CONFUSION

There are many stages that you go through before reaching a professional level of competency. At each stage, there's a tendency to be thrown and to drop what you first learned. When concentrating on vocalizing a song on a single vowel, and then singing the lyrics in that vocal place, the different vowels and consonants will tend to obscure your placement. Be patient: As you continue, the two experiences will come together.

EARNING THE SONG

Many times you'll pick up a song for the first time and sing it spontaneously. Later, when you start to study it, you may have a struggle. This is very common. The Zen Buddhists would say, "At the first try, the song is singing you, not you singing the song." With the first experience, there is a spontaneous inspiration; but as you begin to be more familiar with the song, you tend to lose that inspiration. You will gain the technique to recapture that spontaneity when you become conscious of the real work that has to go into it.

After you have acquired the technique to handle the song, you will have to perform the song in front of an audience at least five or six times, applying the technique, before you can really feel that you have conquered the song. Do your job and forget about the results. Gradually, when you become more aware of the technique that does the job, you will have earned the song. It will have become yours.

ORGANIZATION

The hardest part in studying singing is to get it all together. Many students aspire to be singers, but few can organize themselves to develop as a professional. Organization of time for practicing, for making a living, taking care of an apartment, and so forth are challenges. It is only the determined who will really achieve professionalism. Organization is a talent in itself; many fall by the wayside because of the lack it.

COMMITMENT AND SACRIFICE

To study seriously takes money and time. A lot of students don't have either, but those that have the determination and devotion will eventually succeed. Singing is a highly competitive and precarious profession, so think over your dream and be sure that you can take the work and sacrifice that goes with it.

20

Professional Rehearsal Techniques

Learn how to save your voice.

♪

Becoming professional presents different adjustments in practicing. You have to learn how to save your voice and, at times, continue to sing when not up to par.

TIME OFF

Taking time off one day a week relieves pressures and tensions, allowing you to come back to your studies refreshed. The body gets tense when concentrating on a new technique, so resting is helpful not only to let the voice recuperate but also to relieve the mind. Taking a day off will bring relaxation and ease to your singing.

SICKNESS

Practice when you're not feeling well so long as your vocal folds are not affected. Work the problem through with your teacher. Professionals have to sing when ill and must learn how to handle the voice when it is not up to par; this is vital for a lifelong career. Having a technique for any circumstance is the difference between the amateur and the professional. They can be equally talented, but the professional knows what to do when the voice doesn't respond, whereas the amateur doesn't and gives up.

At the same time, be sure to take rests and not to strain. Stop singing, if you start to cough and choke, or if it hurts. These are signs that the vocal folds are affected. If the vocal folds are affected, do not sing; you can cause permanent damage to your voice. If your condition persists over two weeks, go to an ear, nose, and throat specialist.

MARKING

Marking is a technique used in rehearsal by professionals to save the voice from tiring. Sing all passages softly, as if speaking, dropping an octave lower in higher sections. This brings all of the elements together—voice, music, acting, movement, stage business—without straining the voice.

CHRONIC SORE THROAT

Many singers have persistent allergies that cause chronic throat irritation. Find an expert ear, nose, and throat specialist to keep an eye on you to make sure you are not developing nodes—calluses on the vocal folds. Constant singing on inflamed vocal folds can cause permanent damage.

SAVING TEN PERCENT

The newcomer tends to be like the horse-at-the-gate. The tendency is to try too hard and strain your voice. The professional knows how to reserve the ten percent that gives control both in the singing and acting. Have a commitment, but learn to enjoy the work and let it go once you have done all the preparation. Experience develops this.

SAVING YOUR VOICE

On the day of your performance, don't talk too much. Save your voice and energy for the show. There is a certain ceremony of preparation that you fall into in order to concentrate your physical and mental energy. It is similar to a professional athlete who knows how to gather his strength for the best results.

PSYCHO-CYBERNETICS

Psycho-cybernetics is an excellent technique for practicing when you can't use your voice (see pages 98 to 100).

21

How to Audition

Don't go for the job; go to grow.

℘

Auditioning is part of being professional. Unless you know someone of influence or your spouse is a producer, you can't avoid auditioning. Many performers hate auditioning, but it is necessary to get a job. Therefore, look upon auditioning as a part of your education. Don't go into it haphazardly. Acquire a positive attitude and technique for auditioning, and you can actually grow to like auditions.

WHEN

Although auditioning is a vital necessity, there is a right time for it in your development. You have to be advanced enough in your vocal and acting abilities to audition. Many audition for the experience without being ready, feeling that they need to practice in front of an audience. This is self-defeating since auditors will remember you in a negative way if you do not perform well.

Go to auditions when you and your teacher think you have something specific to offer. Go with a gift: You wouldn't give anyone a half-baked cake. Definite techniques in auditioning will be covered in this chapter that will help you develop the right attitude, preparation, and presentation for an audition.

ATTITUDE

The main reason for auditioning or performing is to share a message with your audience. The message is found in the objective of the scene. For instance, in *The Kiss of the Spider Woman*, when the mother sings the song "You Could Never Shame Me" to her son, her objective is to assure her son that she is not ashamed of his being gay. Find a similar situation in your life and connect it with the objective in the scene. You may choose confronting your real son about his not finding a job. Then you will have the total commitment you need to share that message.

Be thoroughly convinced of this message, and you will find a newly energized concentration that frees you from being self-conscious. When your scene is full—revealing a deep emotional experience—you will have done a good audition. You may or may not get the job, but good auditions are never forgotten. They're like money in the bank; you build a reputation on them (like the interest you earn on your bank deposit). Bad ones are not forgotten either; they leave a poor impression. That's why it is important to be ready to audition; otherwise, when you are finally prepared, the auditioners will see your name and say, "Oh, don't bother with that one."

TECHNIQUE

Many performers say they hate auditioning, admitting that they do much better in performance. Develop a technique for auditioning that helps you perform as well in audition as on stage.

Remember the main attitude in auditioning is to share the message with your audience and not show off your talent. The harder you try to demonstrate your talent, the more empty it will be because you are just displaying yourself. Without a message, you lack emotional conviction. Go for the scene and the technique to fill it; then you will be concentrating on what you want and not how you are doing. Use your vocal and acting technique to express what you have to say. As you perfect your craft, you will have a better chance of getting the job.

PREPARATION

Practice—Master Class

The Master Class is the ideal place to practice performing in front of an audience. Consider the classroom as a place to face your fears, anxieties, reactions, and habits. Go to open mics at piano bars, sing for friends, sing for any- and everybody except auditioners. The aim is to know yourself. Welcome fear: Find what your reaction and technical needs are when you get nervous. In this way, "To know yourself is enlightenment!"

Head Shots

When you are ready to audition, get your photos and prepare your résumé. These will aid the auditioners in identifying you not only when you are auditioning, but also after you have left, when they are making their choices. It is very amateurish to walk into an interview or audition without a photo and résumé, so make sure you have both.

Find a good photographer by asking friends or looking at advertisements in the trade magazines like *Backstage*. Call photographers and make an appointment to see their work. In other words, audition them. Get a simple, good-looking wardrobe, avoiding a lot of patterns or flowers. Have a friend take a roll of Polaroid shots in different outfits to give you an idea of what you look like.

Ask the photographer if he has a makeup and hair person. If not, find one yourself. Pictures are very expensive, so do this legwork before spending your money.

You will need two poses. The first should be a casual shot showing you in simple dress and smiling at the lens; your eyes should say, "Hello." The second should be a theatrical pose with a serious look in a more formal dress. Avoid composite shots of two, three, or four photos together. They are used by character actors or dancers in costume. However, you can use a composite shot for your postcard reminder to agents.

The auditioners are looking for personality and individuality. Bring out your personality by visualizing a specific acting scene in each shot. See your partner in the camera and play an action to him during the shot. This will enliven your pictures and bring a personal depth to them. Auditioners often have hundreds of photos submitted to them. The one that jumps out at them is the one with personality. Don't think of having personality.

Think of the scene and play the action to your partner; this will bring out your personality.

When you get the proofs, show them to someone in the business whose judgment you trust—your teacher or a fellow student—and select the best according to consensus.

Have your name printed at the bottom. Later you can have postcards made to send to agents as reminders that you're alive and waiting for a job. Have your name, unions, and phone number printed on the bottom.

Résumés

Résumés give the auditioner a personal account of your performing experience and educational training. There is a set outline used: Have your name in large letters, centered on the top. On the next line, on the right side, put your height, weight, hair and eye color—list each under the other in a small column. In the left column, at the opposite side of the page, list your unions (SAG, Equity, AFTRA, and so forth). In the middle of the top line under your name, list your type—Ingenue, Character Actor, and so forth (see Figure 21–1).

List your credits, in the order of their importance, under the following categories: Broadway, Off-Broadway, Stock, Television, Commercials (if you have done many commercials, say, "List available on request" to avoid conflict with similar products, etc.). Under each category of show, list the title of the musical or play, the part you played, and the place that you did the role, all on one line.

Next list any Awards you've received, Education, Teachers, and Special Skills (ballroom dancing, water skiing, and so forth). Leave a space on the bottom where you can put your agent's name and phone number. If you have reviews, you can list them on a separate page.

The Audition Package

The basic song choices for auditioning are a ballad and an uptune—a fast tempo song. However, a complete audition package that covers all styles and sounds should consist of nine different styles of songs and two monologues (one serious, one comedic) chosen from the following categories:

Dramatic Ballad–shows your vocal and dramatic range:
1. Broadway Belt (chest voice)
   For example, "If He Walked into My Life" from *Mame*

ANITA BOLTON
Leading Lady

EQUITY
SAG
AFTRA

Height: 5'8"
Weight: 115
Hair: Brown
Eyes: Brown

Broadway

Hello Dolly...Ms. Rose...........................w/Carol Channing
Bye, Bye Birdie................................Mayor's Wife................................AMAS Theater

Off-Broadway

Paris...Vivienne......................Playwrights Foundation
The Meehans..Casey........................Theater for the New City

Regional Theater

Ankles Aweigh..Lucia......................Goodspeed Opera House
Sally Blane, Girl Detective........................Tia....................Bristol Riverside Theater,PA
The Rink..Anna.....................Broadhollow Theater, NY
Chicago...Velma.....................Broadhollow Theater, NY
Carousel...Mrs. Mullins..........Harry Chapin Lakeside Thea.

Television

Commercials and Voiceovers...List on request
As the World Turns..WCBS
One Life to Live..WABC

Cabaret

One Woman Show.......................................Club 88's & Don't Tell Mama

Training

Voice: Arabella Hong Young (10 yrs.)
Jazz Dance: Phil Black
Acting: Berghof Studios, Bill Hickey (8 yrs.)
Commercials: Joyce Barker

Special Skills

Dialects: Italian, French, and Spanish; 3 octave range (legit, pop, and jazz)
drive a motorcycle, water ski, roller skate

FIGURE 21-1. Sample résumé.

2. Broadway Legit (head voice)
  For example, "Till There Was You" from *The Music Man*
3. Rock Belt (chest voice)
  For example, "There Are Worse Things I Could Do" from *Grease*
4. Jazz (chest voice)
  For example, "Something To Live For" from *Sophisticated Ladies*

UPTUNE–a medium or fast tempo generating energy with body movement or choreography:
5. Broadway Belt (chest voice)
  For example, "Lot of Livin" from *Bye, Bye Birdie*
6. Broadway Legit (head voice)
  For example, "Falling In Love with Love" from *The Boys from Syracuse*
7. Rock Belt (chest voice)
  For example, "Magic To Do" from *Pippin*
8. Jazz Swing Tempo (chest voice)
  For example, "The Lady Is a Tramp" from *Babes In Arms*

CHARACTER SONG–humorous, belt voice, fast patter:
  For example, "Don't, 'Ah, Ma' Me" from *The Rink*

TWO MONOLOGUES–one serious and one comedic. Choose monologues to lead into any of the above songs.

The songs chosen above are very famous to make the examples obvious. Try, however, to choose lesser known selections of a similar type. Auditioners get very tired of hearing the same pieces all the time.

Choosing the Song

Sing what you do best. Or, if you're auditioning for a show, sing a song that is closest to the character for whom you are trying out.

If you get a call to audition right away and don't have the proper type of song to sing, you can take a dramatic selection and change your objective to make it humorous. Take the song "Love, Look Away" from *The Flower Drum Song*; your objective may be to end a relationship to protect yourself from being hurt. To make the scene humorous—belittle your lover by laughing him off.

Organization of Materials

Have your routine written down. A *routine* is the order and way in which you sing the song—whether you do cuts (you may cut out the verse and start with the chorus), where you slow down and go back into tempo, what the feel is. The rhythm you want conveys what the feel is. It may be Broadway 2, Samba, slow ballad, and so forth, and should be written on the left side at the top of the music.

In order to present an easy to follow accompaniment, make extra copies of your original music. Cut and paste-up the music in the order that you do it so that the accompanist does not have to go back to repeated sections. The song will read straight through just the way you do it. You may start with the chorus first and then go back to the verse; in this way the music is laid out in the exact way that you sing it. If you have a special ending, be sure that it is written out and placed in the proper spot.

The paste-up is easier for the accompanist to follow for cuts or changes. Lay it out so that it reads straight through, with all dynamic and tempo changes marked in red ink. If you do the song in a different key, be sure you have your key marked in red in the upper left hand corner and tell the accompanist. Also, have all the chord changes written clearly in the right key.

In trying out for a specific show, you must sing in the key written in the original piano vocal score because the orchestration is written in that key.

Finally, when you get a song you sing particularly well, you should have a copyist write the piano part out for you—vocal line and piano part (lead sheets only have the vocal line and chords). The written piano part is expensive but well worth the cost for a smooth audition.

Open Call

For an open call, where the audition is open to everybody, and you don't have to be an Equity member, have a paste-up of the last sixteen bars of the song prepared for the accompanist. (This is usually the last return of the chorus and the ending.) The sixteen-bar audition is common for open calls, but bring the complete song also, in case they want to hear more. At Equity calls, by appointment, they let you sing the complete piece.

When singing a complete song, do not do repeats of verses or choruses unless the song is very fast. Think "Hit 'em hard and fast." The actual song should be no longer than two minutes, as studio time is very expensive and auditioners sometimes have literally hundreds of singers to hear. Make a good impression by being professional and quick.

Dress

Musical theater goes entirely by type casting; therefore, when you go for a specific role, dress to suggest the part, but don't overdo it. If your type, however, is so far from the character, go all the way and get into costume.

Study the Part

If you're going for a specific role, do some research on the character by listening to the original cast album for vocal quality and style (not the movie; the vocal sound can be quite different from the Broadway version). Study the libretto—story line and dialogue—and vocal score at the library. If the musical is not playing at the time, look at the video of the show, even though it may differ from the original. Be sure you get the music from the original vocal score, which is often in a different key than the selections.

PSYCHOLOGICAL PREPARATION AT HOME

Aside from your actual rehearsal schedule, prepare psychologically at home by recalling your message from your scene. Auditioners will believe in your performance when you truly believe in your scene. Forget about competition; think of your convictions in the scene. If you had a bad experience the last time you auditioned, let go of negative thoughts and learn from previous mistakes.

Visualize yourself as you would like to be—fully in your scene with ease and concentration the week previous to auditioning and before the actual audition itself.

Fear

Everyone gets nervous, which is a type of fear. Distinguish between excitement and fear. Excitement is a positive anticipation of the unknown, whereas fear is a lack of confidence in your abilities. Don't run away from your anxieties; they'll just loom larger. There is a tremendous power in fear; use it as the obstacle in your scene, and you will be amazed at the strength it will give you. Review Chapter 18.

Negative Thoughts

Anxiety is the first reaction when self-doubt strikes. Don't be afraid if you get nervous when you have to perform. Remember it's hardest to perform for relatives or those you care a great deal about. Strangers you won't see again, so they don't affect you as much. Concentrate on what you want to do technically, and don't go for making an impression. Remember, bringing a message to the audience is the main reason for performing.

Your first impulse may be to sing to the audience. Don't think of the audience. Bring your scene to the audience, not the audience to your scene. Don't look at the audience; instead see the scene in your mind's eye. When you are truly concentrated in the scene, you will not even notice that the audience is there. Sense the audience but do not concentrate on them directly. Allow them to share your scene like someone listening to a private conversation. Just sensing the audience can lift you to greater heights, because it demands a fuller concentration and stronger intention from you—these moments can lead to inspiration.

Controlling Anxiety a Week Before the Audition
A week before the performance, you can feel your nerves act up while you are simply relaxing, looking at TV, or having a conversation. You may doubt yourself or be haunted by old thoughts like, "Why am I doing this? Why do I want to perform; I get so nervous?!!"

To handle your nerves, review your message and your technique briefly. These thoughts fortify you for the eventual performance. Some people call it "Psyching yourself up." I prefer "Tuning yourself up." When your conviction or message is more important than making an impression, you will start to gain confidence. Guide yourself by using psycho-cybernetics; visualize without making a sound.

Nervousness Before Singing
The first thing that happens when you practice for the audition, is you may get nervous and lose your breath. The BBC exercise on page 86 enables you to breathe abdominally, calms you down, and centers you in order to concentrate. Doing the BBC five times will take less than a minute, releasing tensions and strengthening you. Don't will it; let it happen.

Use Your Gift
Use the gift with which you were born. This attitude will give you strength because you will be recognizing that you have the talent and need only apply the technique of the self and voice to use that talent. Pray to whatever Power you believe in: "Help me be what I am."

Practice Auditioning

Take at least two weeks to prepare for the audition if you can. Practice by performing for any and everybody—in class, for friends, at showcases. Do a series of auditions; let auditioning be par for the course.

PSYCHOLOGICAL PREPARATION
IN THE WAITING ROOM

Five minutes before they call you, review your scene intentions (objective, obstacle, actions, and so forth) psycho-cybernetically. Review your personal substitution for the scene for a deep emotional commitment with a strong beginning and ending. The first and last impression are the most important. Starting weak makes it hard to regain the auditioner's interest; ending hesitantly, usually at the climax of the song, leaves a bad impression.

THE AUDITION

Personal Presentation

You are auditioning the minute you enter the room until the time you leave. How you walk, stand, introduce yourself, and give the tempo to the accompanist shows what kind of person you are. Let it be gracious and efficient.

TIPS ON PRESENTING YOURSELF:

Entrance: Enter and greet the auditioners as friends in your living room.

Attitude: Think, "I'm glad you're looking for someone my type."

Greeting: Say, "Hello, I'm _____. I would like to sing _____ for you."

Most often there is an accompanist; but if you have a special arrangement, bring a recorded accompaniment. Nevertheless, some auditioners do not allow recorded accompaniments, so ask, "I have a special arrangement; would you mind if I use a recording?" Be sure to bring your sheet music in case they say, "No." At an important audition, bring your own accompanist.

Performance

After greeting the auditioners, give the music to the accompanist. Set the tempo by singing the first part of the melody in a quiet range. Let the accompanist know if you have any changes in tempo. It should take thirty seconds and no more because all your routine markings have been indicated in red.

Next, scan the room, moving to the center of the space—not too close and not too far from the auditioners. If you stand too close, they can't see you objectively; if you stand too far away, it looks as if you're afraid of them. On a large stage, stand in the midapron (downstage) in the light.

Before you start the song, adjust your body stance to your physical life in the scene, see your surroundings in the scene and address your partner. Most students tend to stand in a rigid, upright position ready to perform. Instead, put your partner downstage and have your eye focus at the level of the auditioners' eyes. Don't look at the auditioners; focus between their heads, or put your imaginary partner about eight feet in front of you. Don't focus in midair. Find a spot or use a chair to place your imaginary partner. See your partner—in your mind's eye—to help you concentrate and to keep your eyes from blinking. Let your partner be spontaneous, allowing him to move around in your mind. Auditioners don't want to be in the scene; they want to observe. Singing to them, makes them feel that they have to respond. There is an exception: In an audience piece, use them as part of the scene.

Many students drop their eyes and stare at the floor, listening for their musical cue. During the piano introduction, get your eyes off the floor. Focus on your partner. Let him evoke a physical reaction from you (a shrug of the shoulders, a smile). This should propel you into the first line of your song.

Go for the objective in your scene. Don't bring the audition to your scene; bring your scene to the audition. Don't see the auditioners; see the fourth wall and your partner.

After you have sung, pause. Unless they talk to you, say, "Thank you." with a smile and exit. Leave quickly in a friendly way; don't hang around for comments. Don't apologize if you didn't sing well.

Call Backs

If you get a call back (say a prayer of thanks!), try to sing the actual song from the show. This will give a better idea of how you would be in the part. If you sing the same song, go with a deeper emotional experience. Stage directions are only for the actual setup of the play. Don't use them unless they are important, like running out of a room.

Age

If your part calls for an older or younger person, play age by imagining a partner who brings out that particular age in you. We become a different person and age, depending on the person to whom we are speaking. For example, I will be older and more authoritative with my students, but younger when I speak to my father who is 101 years old.

Extreme old age is portrayed by pinpointing infirmities. If your back has ever gone out, you know how it is to favor it in a specific spot and how you can't straighten up when you try to walk. Use this experience.

Summer Stock

Trying for summer stock, play the character as it is usually played, internalizing your own interpretation. With little rehearsal time, oftentimes only one week, the director is anxious to get the show on the boards. He doesn't have time to develop your special interpretation.

Take the audition as a chance to learn. After the audition, write down the good things you have done and the points you need to correct. Don't be discouraged if you don't get the job. Most parts are type cast, and you have to fit into the picture. You need to be visually and vocally compatible with the other players.

Summary

Auditioning is not just singing a song, you offer the fullest range of yourself as a person, artist, and professional. This is shown by:

1. Your choice of material—showing vocal range, depth as an artist, and stylistic versatility
2. Your presentation as a person—as seen in your résumé and friendly, professional attitude
3. Your actual performance—revealing vocal and acting skills with a deep emotional commitment

At an interview, the famous choreographer Bob Fosse said that he keeps everybody who dances well, regardless of how they look. Afterward, he asks them to sing; when they do a song they know, he says you can generally tell whether there's something inside.

That something inside is the message. Remember, as Michael Shurtleff stated in his book on auditioning, "It's better to be strong and wrong than weak and dull."

Chapter Twenty-one

So, the essence of auditioning is to have a message.

> When you have a message, you will be enlightened.
> Share that message, and you will be an artist.
> When you are an artist, you will get the job.
> Don't try to prove yourself; don't go for the job.

GO TO GROW!

Summary
of
Vocalises

The Chest Voice Exercises

LOWER

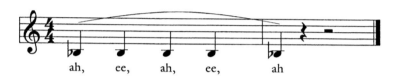

Vocalising *ah* and *ee*

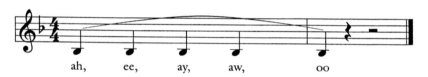

The Vowel Circle

HIGHER

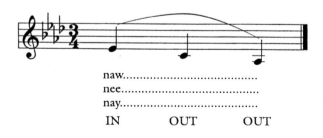

The Fifth

yah.......................
yee.......................
yay.......................
yaw.......................
yoo.......................

Octave Drop in Chest Voice

The Legitimate Head Voice Exercises in the Middle Range

hm nee........................   naw.......................................

Three Note Scale

hm nee...............................nah.........................

Five Note Scale

hmnee,ah,ee,ah,ee,ah,ee,ah,ee nee,ah,ee,ah,ee,ah,ee,ah,ee

Scale of Thirds

The Mask Technique

LEGITIMATE

nyaghm, nyaghm, nyaghm, nyaghm, nyaghm

Descending Fifth on *Nyaghm*

SIMULATED BELT VOICE

nyaghm, nyaghm, nyaghm, nyaghm, nyaghm

Descending Fifth on *Nyaghm*

Singing on the Breath

Octave Leap for *Noo*

Octave Leap on *Noo* with *Ee* Turn

Tonal Control

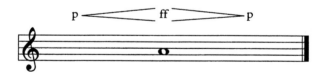

Messa di Voce

Exercise for the High Register

see........................yay........—..............

Octave and a Third

Exercise for the Extreme High Register

see.....................yay...........................

Octave and a Third

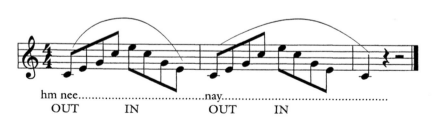

hm nee............................nay...................................
    OUT   IN   OUT   IN

Lower Octave and the Third

Coloratura

FAST RUNS

hm nee.........................ay..

OUT..........................IN....................................

The Octave and the Fourth Scale

RAPID PASSAGES

FAST

nee...

yah........yah........yah.......yah.................yah.......yah........yah

Sixteenth Note Figures

TRILLS

Whole Note Trill

Turns and Grace Notes

Falsetto

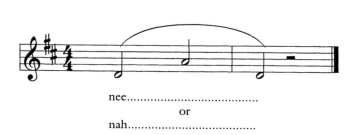

Falsetto Exercise for Males